ROTARY IN CALGARY

ROTARY IN CALGARY

Celebrating One Hundred Years

FRED STENSON

Published in Canada by Kingsley Publishing
www.kingsleypublishing.ca

Cover and interior design: Kisscut Design

Front cover images: Ferris Wheel © Madeline Krentz;
Chuckwagon at Heritage Park © Jason Cheever /
Dreamstime.com; Windmill © Alex Evans / Dreamstime.
com; Sunflower © Jason Cheng / Dreamstime.com;
Calgary Tower © Ian Whitworth / Dreamstime.com;
Rotary Bell © Heather Simonds; Feathers for a Pow Wow
at Indian Village © Jason Cheever / Dreamstime.com;
Rotary Challenger Park Statue © Malcolm Wilcox;
Peace Bridge © Jeff Whyte / Dreamstime.com; Globe ©
Rabbitsfoot / Dreamstime.com; Bicycle © Sasilsolutions /
Dreamstime.com

Printed in Canada by Friesens

2014/1
First Edition

Library and Archives Canada Cataloguing in Publication

Stenson, Fred, 1951–, author
Rotary in Calgary : celebrating one hundred years /
Fred Stenson.

Includes bibliographical references and index.
ISBN 978-1-926832-24-1 (bound)

1. Rotary Club of Calgary — History.
2. Rotary Club of Calgary — Pictorial works.
I. Title.

HF5001.R83C3 2014   369.5'209712338   C2014-901137-7

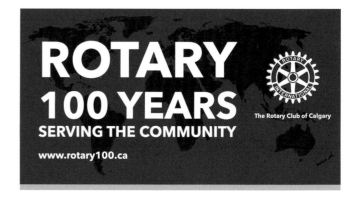

CONTENTS

ON BEHALF OF THE GOVERNMENT OF ALBERTA, it is my pleasure to provide greetings to The Rotary Club of Calgary on your one-hundredth anniversary.

One hundred years is an incredible milestone. Through each of these years, Rotarians have come together through commitment and fellowship to contribute to a better Calgary and a better world through significant service. As we build provincial economic strength and diversity, success cannot be attained without paralleled social and cultural growth. Whether serving your club, vocation, community, or an international project, I want to express my appreciation for the work that you have done to help build more inclusive, engaged, and sustainable communities.

I hope this centennial year is one of great pride as you reflect on your spirit of generosity and many accomplishments.

ALISON M. REDFORD, QC
Premier of Alberta

ON BEHALF OF THE CITIZENS OF CALGARY and my
City Council colleagues, I congratulate The Rotary Club
of Calgary on one hundred years of service to our city.

Over the past century, The Rotary Club of Calgary has
been a model for other service organizations. Time and
again, Rotarians have come together to fulfill an unmet
need in our community. From their early years and
creating the Boys' Club for those whose fathers had
gone off to war, to recently helping establish the Rotary/
Flames House and the Rotary/Flames Park for families
who are going through challenging times, The Rotary
Club of Calgary has been leading the way.

It is difficult to imagine our city without the contributions of The Rotary Club of Calgary and its members,
if only because they have been so effective at spreading
their message and being models of active citizenship to
all Calgarians. We are a much better place for having
The Rotary Club of Calgary in our city, and I look forward
to seeing what the next hundred years of "Service Above
Self" will bring.

Sincerely,

NAHEED K. NENSHI
Mayor

Linda and Pat Killoran

IT IS MY DISTINCT PLEASURE as District governor to congratulate The Rotary Club of Calgary for one hundred years of service to Calgary, the District, and the world. I applaud the concept of this book as a way to record and share this wonderful history in a way that combines celebration with storytelling.

There are no doubt many events and projects that help define this past one hundred years. However, none of these would be possible without the strong leadership and vibrant membership that has characterized this club over those one hundred years. There are many stories and people that should make us all proud.

The growth and prosperity of this club has allowed Rotarians to enhance the lives of Calgarians, Albertans, and the citizens of the world. The world is a better place because The Rotary Club of Calgary has been in our midst, at work, improving our communities, and helping our citizens.

Congratulations for one hundred years of service and for this book, which captures the moments that demonstrate why The Rotary Club of Calgary is special.

Enjoy!

PATRICK (PAT) KILLORAN
District Governor 2013–14

CONGRATULATIONS Rotary Club of Calgary on achieving a milestone—one hundred years of service above self!

We've come a long way from our first organizing meeting in the Hudson's Bay Company restaurant on March 18, 1914, to our charter celebration on May 3, 2014, in the Hyatt Hotel.

From raising $2,000 annually for community projects to raising more than $1 million annually for community projects.

From being the first and only club in Calgary to being one of thirteen vibrant and growing clubs serving a great city, including members of all ages, genders, and backgrounds who share a common love of fellowship and a belief in the duty to serve our community.

From planting trees at the Public Library to building parks and bicycle pathways—in collaboration with all Calgary Rotary Clubs—that will encircle our city via the legacy Rotary Mattamy Greenway Project.

From bringing the first kangaroo to the Calgary Zoo (1922) to helping flood victims obtain housing after Calgary's worst natural disaster (2013).

Through our one hundred-year journey some things have not changed.

For one hundred years the Palliser Hotel has been our home. Thank you to the good folks of the Palliser!

From our first minstrel show in 1917 we continue to sing: at meetings and at our annual President's Ball and Show, a fellowship event that is second to none!

From $5 lunches in the 1920s to $40 lunches today, we continue to complain about the cost of lunch.

We believe passionately in serving our community, locally and around the world. "Service Above Self" has been our motto for one hundred years.

Rotary operates in a very different environment today than it did one hundred years ago. But the purpose of Rotary has never been more relevant. In today's fast-paced world of endless information, instant communication, and increased complexity, there is a hunger for meaningful fellowship, connection with others, and making a difference.

It is our pleasure to serve as the board of this great club during the centennial year. As we celebrate our club's one-hundredth year, we remember the leadership of those who came before, and we commit to build on the foundation laid by them for service to community.

EVA FRIESEN, *President* | PAUL BATES, *Director, International Service, Vice-president* | DOUG MACDONALD, *Past President* | BARBARA BURGRAFF, *Director, Community Service* | RON ESCH, *Incoming President* | KIM VAN VLEIT, *Director, Fundraising* | BARBARA YOUNG, *Co-Secretary* | RALPH LUNDBERG, *Director, Program* | CHRIS HARPER, *Co-Secretary* | PAUL MCINTYRE ROYSTON, *Director, Communications* | DON DART, *Treasurer* | KEN MORAES, *Director, Fellowship* | SID MARK, *Director, Youth* | ROB BROOKWELL, *Director, Membership*

FOREWORD

PEOPLE OFTEN ASK ME, "What is Rotary?" I now have an answer for them: "Read this book!" *Rotary in Calgary: Celebrating One Hundred Years* will inform, entertain, and inspire you. It tells the story of courageous men and women who gave and continue to give their time and energy to countless people throughout the world. You will wish that you could be a part of it. The good news is, you can.

Rotary Clubs were initiated by Paul Harris, a lonely young lawyer who longed for the companionship of colleagues in the business world. He invited men from different careers to meet with him for lunch. From those first meetings in Chicago, Rotary was born. The idea grew, and spread to Calgary in 1914.

In 1952, I was secretary to the maître d' and assistant manager of Calgary's Palliser Hotel when Merrill Huntley resigned as executive secretary of The Rotary Club of Calgary. Rotarians offered me the position. I accepted, and it changed my life.

Club members liked to tease me when the club's only eligible bachelor, G. H. Curly Galbraith, drove me home after work. In 1954, the club asked me to attend the International Rotary Convention in Seattle and suggested Curly provide my transportation. I understand that behind the scene bets were placed that we would be married within a year, and we were!

Curly soon became club president, then District governor, and in 1988 was elected vice-president of Rotary International. I, of course, accompanied him on his travels and learned of the many worthwhile projects being undertaken by clubs around the world.

One of my favourite memories was when Curly and I visited Fiji and he was asked to speak to the club. Only two or three members showed up, but Curly talked to them about all the fine work being done by clubs around the world. Ten years later, a man approached Curly at a function and told him he had been present at that meeting in Fiji, which had been held for the purpose of turning in the club's charter. After Curly's talk, members changed their minds and decided to continue. They remain a vibrant club with many members to this day. Curly and I were often gratified to see how even small clubs could have an impact on their community and the world through their projects.

Some readers of this book may recall the many interesting members of the Calgary club over the years. Kibitzing between Archdeacon "Swanny" Swanson and Dr. Frank Morley, minister at Grace Presbyterian Church, brought many a laugh, as did the pranks of fellows like Bill Tynan and Don Cushing, who dressed as Hutterites and presented a rubber chicken to the president, accusing him of running over it and asking for recompense. We even had a Stunt Committee; no one knew who would be the brunt of the "joke of the day" until it was enacted. Birthdays were recognized, often with a bio of the celebrant. When members welcomed a new baby into their family, Rotarians took up a collection and presented it to the proud papa.

But it wasn't all fun and games. The Calgary club donated more than they were asked to the Rotary International Polio Fund, which helped the World Health Organization nearly eradicate polio worldwide. Many Rotarians actually travelled to Third World countries and administered the vaccine.

Members donned their jeans and removed debris from highway ditches. They sponsored a golf tournament that raised thousands of dollars for the Stay-in-School Committee. Rotarians become mentors for students. The Rotary Stampede Barbecue, instituted many years ago, is still going strong and has raised millions of dollars for charities.

Rotary and Calgary grew up together. This is the story of that relationship and of the men and women who cemented the friendship.

DORIS GALBRAITH
2014

DORIS AND CURLY GALBRAITH on their fiftieth wedding anniversary, 2005.

Rotary Comes TO Calgary

1

THE ROTARY CLUB OF CALGARY was the ninth Rotary Club chartered in Canada. What is startling, in terms of how fast the Rotary movement was spreading, was that only nine years separated the birth of Rotary in Chicago in 1905 and the formation of the first Calgary club in 1914. Calgary's club was part of Rotary's frontier: one of the first two hundred clubs of what is now over thirty-four thousand clubs worldwide.

ROTARY'S LOGO is a wheel with cogs. Meshed with many other wheels, it can turn the world.

IN 1905, PAUL HARRIS founded the Rotary movement. He is seen here with his wife, Jean, later in life.

ROTARY WAS THE BRAINCHILD OF PAUL HARRIS.
Born in Wisconsin, Harris was raised by paternal grandparents in a small town in Vermont. He became a lawyer — a career that led him to Chicago. He found the city a lonely place and one day, while walking with a fellow lawyer who was a native of Chicago, he was struck by how his colleague knew all the shopkeepers along the street well enough to stop and talk to them. Harris's own life in the city lacked such connections. In his memoir, *My Road to Rotary*, Harris wrote,

> The thought persisted that I was experiencing only what had happened to hundreds, perhaps thousands, of others in a big city . . . I was sure that there must be many other young men who had come from farms and small villages to establish themselves in Chicago . . . Why not bring them together? If others were longing for fellowship as I was, something would come of it.

As a starting point, Paul Harris told a few of his business associates that he wanted to create an organization of professionals who would meet for fellowship and collaboration. On February 23, 1905, Harris and three others met and discussed the idea. By the third meeting, the group was bigger and the organization had formed to the extent of having a president: Silvester Schiele. Paul Harris would take his turn as president in Rotary's third year.

The name Rotary came from the practice of rotating among the members' offices for the weekly meeting. The image chosen to represent Rotary was a wheel with cogs. The organization was a drive wheel that, when meshed with the cogs of other wheels, could drive more and more social activity.

Rotary is described as the world's first service club. It began with the idea of fellowship, but, in 1907, the club performed its first act of community service when it worked to install public toilets in Chicago. This was sure to inspire a joke or two, but the need was serious, and the action greatly improved the city's sanitation.

The drive to extend Rotary to other cities came from Paul Harris, but some who liked the idea of Rotary being solely a Chicago club resisted. Harris won out, and the second Rotary Club was formed in San Francisco in 1908. After five years, Rotary Clubs existed in several U.S. cities, and, in 1910, with sixteen clubs, Rotary held its first conference of the National Association of Rotary Clubs. A speech by A. F. Sheldon at the first conference of this association contained the sentence: "He profits most who serves his fellows best." At the second Rotary conference in Portland, Oregon, Sheldon's statement turned into Rotary's motto. Those who preferred something shorter inspired the motto that has lasted to this day: "Service Above Self."

Rotary came to Canada in 1912 when a Winnipeg club (the thirty-fifth Rotary Club) was organized. It was the first time a Rotary Club had existed outside of the U.S., and the association of clubs became known as the International Association of Rotary Clubs. In 1922, this was changed to Rotary International (RI).

In the winter of 1913–14, a group in Calgary began to bat around the idea of a Rotary Club for the city. Tom Weir, local manager of the Remington Typewriter Company, had heard about Rotary through a friend in Denver. Weir contacted Rotary headquarters in Chicago to find out how a new club was formed. About the same time, Jim Giffen, manager of R. C. Dunn and Company in Vancouver, gave his company's Calgary manager, Jim Ryan, a pep talk on the organization. The International secretary of Rotary suggested that Ryan get in touch with Tom Weir. They became friends. William (Bill) Ardern and Doug Howland were also involved in the early discussion group.

Bill Ardern contacted Bill Pease, president of the Toronto Rotary Club, and Pease wrote back, "A Rotary Club would be a good thing. It would make a real town out of Calgary."

Much of the early history of Calgary's first Rotary Club revolves around the Lougheed Building on 1st Street and 6th Avenue SW. Constructed in 1912, the Lougheed is an L-shaped office block angled around the Grand Theatre. The building and theatre were owned by, and named for, lawyer and businessman James Lougheed, grandfather of Peter Lougheed who was Alberta's popular premier from 1971 to 1985. James Lougheed was government senate leader in 1913 and would soon be knighted by George V (1916). He was as powerful a figure as existed in frontier Calgary and owned a great deal of real estate. As a lawyer, one of his main clients was the Canadian

THE LOUGHEED BUILDING (and Grand Theatre) in 2013. The Rotary Club of Calgary's first office was room 333.

Pacific Railway (CPR). The Grand Theatre was one of several theatres he owned in western Canada.

In the basement of the Lougheed Building was a restaurant called Cronn's Rathskeller. It was arguably Calgary's most popular restaurant of the day. One reason was that lunch cost thirty-five cents, compared to fifty cents down the street at the Hudson's Bay Company. An important planning meeting to start a Calgary Rotary Club took place at Cronn's on February 16, 1914. Tom Weir, Jim Ryan, Bill Ardern, and Doug Howland were present — and so were Phil McCrystle and Fred Harling, both of whom had shops in the Lougheed Building. McCrystle was a tailor and Harling ran a women's clothing store. The group decided membership in their club would cost $10.

The official founding meeting of The Rotary Club of Calgary took place on March 18, 1914, at the Elizabethan Dining Room in the Hudson's Bay Company store. Club history states that sixty-four members attended. The March 19, 1914, *Calgary Herald** quibbled with that number, claiming "forty members enrolled." Right or wrong on that point, the *Herald* did history the favour of listing the committee members that would support the first club president, James S. Ryan. The first vice-president was Bill Watson, and the first secretary-treasurer was Doug Howland. The committee members were as follows:

Bylaws Committee:
F. Shouldice, Tom Weir, and E. E. Vincent

Membership Committee:
W. Ardern, H. Murray, and J. B. Kellyway

Permanent Organization Committee:
P. W. McCrystle, D. E. Black, A. Miller, J. J. MacDonald, and D. W. Howland

* At this time, the *Calgary Herald* was called the *Calgary Daily Herald*.

The *Herald* article went on to report the "objects of the club" as set forth on the membership card:

To promote the recognition of the worthiness of all legitimate occupations and to dignify each member's occupation as affording him an opportunity to serve society.

To encourage high ethical standards in business and professions.

To increase the efficiency of each member by the exchange of ideas and business methods.

To promote acquaintance and an opportunity for service and an aid to success.

To quicken the interest of each member in the public wellbeing, and to cooperate with others in civic development.

JAMES S. RYAN, first president of The Rotary Club of Calgary in 1914: "a ball of fire."

After Jim Ryan had explained the objects of the club, he called on Phil McCrystle to elaborate. Long-time club historian Malcolm McAra described the talk this way:

> The first speaker to address a luncheon meeting of Calgary's Rotary Club was Phil McCrystle. Phil was one of the founding members, a local tailor, and from all accounts his speech indicated he knew as little about Rotary as the sixty members who were listening to him. He talked about everything under the sun except Rotary, of which he knew practically nothing. The few remarks by Fred Shouldice and Jim Ryan after the speech indicated they knew as much about Rotary as McCrystle.

As club historian, Malcolm McAra created a series of "Presidential Profiles." Of first president, Jim Ryan, he wrote: "Ryan proved to be a real 'ball of fire' and soon those men who had signed as members began to appreciate what it meant to be Rotarians."

· · ·

THE ACTIVITIES OF THE CLUB in its first year included a vacant lots garden club, planting trees, assisting the tubercular hospital, and holding the first Rotary picnic in Bowness Park. The club also set up lights so there could be night skating at Elbow Park and provided hampers to the needy at Christmas.

Jim Ryan was married that year, and part of the Ryans' honeymoon was to attend the International Association of Rotary Clubs conference in Houston, Texas. They attended the following year as well, when the International Association of Rotary Clubs organized the member clubs into districts. District 18 contained Calgary, Vancouver, Victoria,

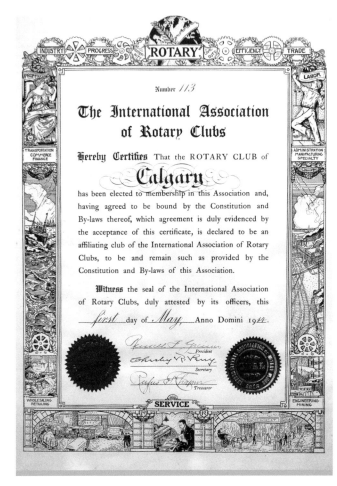

THE ORIGINAL CHARTER of The Rotary Club of Calgary. It was the ninth club in Canada and among the first two hundred Rotary Clubs worldwide.

and Winnipeg. Jim Ryan was the first governor of District 18, and under his administration three new clubs were formed: Edmonton, Fort William/Port Arthur, and Moose Jaw.

Donald B. Smith's book *Calgary's Grand Theatre* tells us more about the relationship between Rotary and the Lougheed Building. It was in the Lougheed that The Rotary Club of Calgary rented its first office: number 333. One floor down, future Rotary president Jeff Lydiatt occupied 205. Lydiatt had begun work for

James Lougheed as personal representative in his theatre enterprises. In December 1914, he became the permanent manager of the Grand Theatre, replacing Bill Sherman.

It seems likely that Jeff Lydiatt lured James Wheeler Davidson into Calgary's Rotary Club, via the Grand Theatre. The two men were directors of Calgary's Symphony Orchestra, when the orchestra had its first-ever performance in the Grand Theatre in November 1913. Jeff Lydiatt joined Calgary's Rotary Club not as a founding member but shortly after. Soon, Jim Davidson joined as well. Both men were early presidents of the club and would go on to become directors of the International Association of Rotary Clubs.

The Rotary Club of Calgary, as it was born in 1914, had many of the ingredients that have kept the club alive and vibrant for one hundred years. First, the club was downtown, close to the action. Next, its members were cultural, political, educational, and business leaders who wanted something more than their business day provided: more friendship, more fun, and more meaning-ful involvement with their community and city. At every stage of the club's life, the same desire for fellowship and service have kept the club energized and enjoyable enough to move on to fresh achievements.

AS OF 2014, The Rotary Club of Calgary has been synonymous with Calgary's downtown for one hundred years.

Building A "Real Town"

2

WHEN BILL PEASE, president of the Rotary Club of Toronto, said in a letter to Calgary's Bill Ardern that "a Rotary Club would make a real town out of Calgary," it might have been fighting words to those Calgarians who believed they already lived in "a real town," but, in the longer run of history, the statement proved true. Calgary was a very young city in 1914, and experiencing a sudden bust after a ten-year boom. Rotary proceeded to make a solid difference in how the city would grow from then on.

THE CONFLUENCE OF THE Elbow and Bow Rivers took its first step in an urban direction when the North West Mounted Police built Fort Calgary in 1875, to stop local whisky trading. A settlement developed across the Elbow River from the fort: a straggle of cabins and stores, whose population supplied and served the Mounties.

Not much changed until the 1880s when it was learned that Calgary would be a station on the Canadian Pacific Railway. In 1883, when the first steam train huffed in, a tent-town stood waiting. The railway company tricked the local speculators by placing Calgary's station a mile west of the old settlement. The Calgary Tower on the skyline of modern Calgary forever signals the position of the original station.

With the arrival of the railway, Calgary's population sprang to four thousand — a size it would maintain until the new century. Wilfrid Laurier's push to fill the prairies with farmers caused Calgary to surge again. The population jumped from four thousand to forty thousand by 1911.

Because of a disastrous fire in 1886 that nearly wiped out the old wooden town, Calgary officials recommended that civic buildings be made of brick or stone. Yellow sandstone was locally available and, from that material, many of Calgary's early buildings and better homes were built — so much so that Calgary became known as "the sandstone city."

After a surge of growth, Calgary began to falter in 1913. As local businessmen were meeting about a Rotary Club for Calgary, the city's real estate boom was collapsing. Even the supply of local sandstone had waned.

Still, the birth year of The Rotary Club of Calgary, 1914, managed to be tumultuous. Two months after the club was chartered, local entrepreneur Archibald Dingman struck wet gas at Turner Valley, and the discovery touched off a stock frenzy. In front of the newly minted Palliser Hotel, boomers stood under placards advertising stacks of Turner Valley stock certificates of dubious value. The sudden oil rush became irrelevant on July 28, 1914, when World War I exploded. Britain declared war on Germany, and Canada followed its mother country into war.

FORT CALGARY was built in 1875 to shut down whisky traders operating on the Bow and Elbow Rivers. This was the origin of Calgary: village, town, and city.
WHEN THE CANADIAN PACIFIC RAILWAY (CPR) arrived in Calgary in 1883, it was a "town of tents." A year later, it had 250 permanent buildings.

EARLY CALGARY WAS CALLED "the sandstone city," and this view of Stephen Avenue shows why.

BUILT IN 1891 for James and Isabella Lougheed, the sandstone mansion (seen below) and its gardens were restored after 1995. Lougheed House was opened to the public in 2005.

WHEN CALGARY'S BUILDING BOOM FALTERED it became obvious how raw the frontier city still was beyond its sandstone centre. Calgary's Rotary Club set out to beautify the city and to build improvements the city and provincial governments were not yet interested in tackling. It is surprising how much that entailed.

One item the local governments were uninterested in supporting were roads beyond Calgary's boundaries. The City was unable, as well, to keep up with the need for trees, gardens, and playgrounds.

Early records suggest that the first Rotary projects in Calgary (unrelated to the war) were tree planting and gardening. Some of the trees planted by the original club members are still alive. For example, in Calgary's Central Memorial Park, Calgary Rotarians planted the giant evergreens in front of the 1912 Memorial Park Library before 1920.

Rotarians were also active on the north side of the Bow River. Between Louise Bridge and Centre Street, the club planted the trees that still shade the riverside path. Rotary also gardened in Calgary's vacant lots during the war, producing much-needed food.

Among Calgary's early Rotarians were a number of automobile enthusiasts. The first "horseless carriage" came to Alberta in 1901. By 1906, when the Province passed its first Automobile Act, there were still only forty-one privately owned cars. Driving became much more popular soon after, but the Province remained reluctant to provide car-worthy roads. It was 1922 before the provincial government began sharing the cost of road building with municipalities. For a long time, the only rural road fit for automobile touring was Calgary to Edmonton — a journey that took two days.

The response of drivers was to form a chapter of the Good Roads Association. James Wheeler Davidson connected Rotary and the Good Roads Association by being an influential member of both. Together, they pushed to have a drivable automobile road between Calgary and Banff. They also lobbied for a road south to the United States. Rotary and the Good Roads Association (which became the Alberta Motor Association) were well ahead of the province in seeing the tourist potential these roads would unlock.

To make the road between Calgary and Banff more attractive, the club decided to plant flowers along it. Rotary historian Malcolm McAra continues the story:

> A cavalcade of cars set out. At designated spots, ground was spaded and planted with poppy seeds. The rains came, the poppies sprouted, and in time bloomed. A magnificent sight: reds, yellows, and whites. And then disaster struck. We had not been aware that deer considered poppies a most delicious and delectable dish. It was very soon noised around that poppies were available, and deer came down from the hills and ate them all up.

Fred Green was chairman of Rotary's poppy-planting committee, and, lest history record that this "good idea" was Rotary's alone, the board minutes of March 20, 1922, state that it was a co-production with Kiwanis and the Good Roads Association. As roads out of Calgary improved, the club installed a Rotary sign at every entrance to the city.

The Rotary Club of Calgary's next building schemes focused on outdoor recreation for young people. First came a campground, then playgrounds.

THE CALGARY-BANFF HIGHWAY in the 1910s. One of the early Calgary Rotary Club's projects was to improve and beautify this road. Rotarians worked in conjunction with the Good Roads Association (ancestor of the Alberta Motor Association).

THE CALGARY EXHIBITION AND STAMPEDE

During its growth and development, the city of Calgary has benefitted greatly from the Calgary Exhibition and Stampede. The Calgary Stampede and the original Calgary Rotary Club are like siblings created by the avid volunteerism of Calgarians. Nowhere was this more visible than during the Calgary flood of 2013, when the population — already overwhelmed by the terrific damage done to many neighbourhoods — came out in their thousands to ensure that the Calgary Stampede would not be cancelled. Thanks to Calgarians' willingness to work, the Calgary Stampede took place on schedule.

The relationship between The Rotary Club of Calgary and the Calgary Exhibition and Stampede was guaranteed the day the Calgary Exhibition hired Ernie Richardson as assistant-exhibition manager in 1903. Ernie Richardson replaced C. W. Peterson as exhibition manager in 1907, in time to oversee Calgary's Dominion Exhibition of 1908. Richardson also introduced Guy Weadick's Calgary Stampede in 1912. It was also Ernie Richardson who administered the marriage of the Calgary Exhibition to the Calgary Stampede in 1923.

Meanwhile, Richardson joined The Rotary Club of Calgary and became one of its mainstays. He was club president in 1932–33.

Calgarians wanting to serve their city have tended to belong to the Calgary Board of Trade (Calgary Chamber of Commerce after 1950), the board of the Calgary Exhibition and Stampede, and The Rotary Club of Calgary. David E. Black, president of Henry Birks and Sons (Western) Ltd. from 1920 to 1951, was a city councillor, a Calgary Stampede Board director, a member of the Board of Trade, and president of The Rotary Club of Calgary. Nat Christie served on the board of Calgary's Rotary Club and was president of the Calgary Exhibition and Stampede from 1926 to 1932.

Other club members who have been president of the Stampede Board are T. A. Hornibrook, Reuban Ward, A. H. McGuire, George E. Edworthy, Gordon H. Love, Charles Kennedy, Ken Moore, Jack Steen, George Brookman, and Steve Allan. Harry Hays may have outdone everyone, having been president of The Rotary Club of Calgary in 1958–59, mayor of Calgary in 1959, a Liberal MP in 1963, and appointed to the Senate in 1966 — plus having been a director of the Calgary Exhibition and Stampede three times (and a life director thereafter).

The upshot is that the two entities, Rotary and the Stampede, have usually pulled in the same direction, trying to make Calgary a great and entertaining place to live, while boosting it as a place to visit and do business. A key year in this process was 1923, when the Exhibition and Stampede merged. To celebrate the fact that his Stampede was now officially Calgary's Stampede, Guy Weadick instituted a new sport, chuckwagon-racing, and asked Calgarians to go western in support of the Stampede. This was the first year that downtown businessmen dressed in jeans and boots and decorated their storefronts with hay bales and slabs. A cowboy, Eddie King, did more than his part to effect the union of downtown and Stampede when he rode his horse into the Club Café on 8th Avenue, did a turn through the kitchen, and out through the dining tables.

Chuckwagon breakfasts remain a big feature of the Calgary Stampede and also trace back to 1923 when Guy Weadick coaxed camp cooks from the big ranches to bring their rigs to the city and serve up beans and flapjacks. Another first, with big significance for The Rotary Club of Calgary, was the buffalo barbecue that ended the 1923 Stampede. Five federal government bison were turned into sandwiches in what was perhaps an ancestor of the club's Stampede Barbecues in the fifties and onwards.

Ernie Richardson applied the same organizing, publicizing, and gathering talents to Rotary that he employed with his Exhibition and finally his Stampede. As chairman of the Educational Committee in 1921, he decided to help Rotary families get to know one another better. He divided the city into seven residential areas. At eight o'clock on the chosen evening, one couple in each area left home and went to the closest Rotarian's home for a visit. When they left, they took their hosts with them and proceeded to the next Rotarian home. This went on all over the city. As can be imagined, the groups grew quickly. Eventually, everyone in each vicinity was gathered into one house — but still the party was not over. The big groups gathered into even bigger groups. The grand finale, all the groups in one house, was realized in the home of alderman and Rotarian G. H. Webster. In the *Rotarian* article describing this feat of fellowship, it was estimated that 150 homes had been called upon that night. "Today every Rotarian family is well acquainted with everybody connected to the club."

Ernie Richardson shocked The Rotary Club of Calgary and the Calgary Exhibition and Stampede with his retirement in 1940. He and his wife moved to North Vancouver, where Ernie actively gardened until his death in 1952.

In 1922, the club leased property on the Elbow River for a campground. The forested area was off the city's southwest corner, upstream and across the Elbow valley from the Calgary Golf and Country Club. The land was leased from a woman in England, through the intermediary, J. H. Goodwin. Dr. Michael Copps Costello, Calgary's mayor from 1915 to 1919, acted with fellow Rotarian Nat Christie on the negotiation of a three-year lease to the end of 1925.

In early 1922, this "permanent camp" was announced to club members. A request was made for subscriptions for a building there, and members fessed up the funds. In June, construction began on what would be humbly known as the "Rotary hut." We know the Rotary campground was in use during the summer of 1923 because a letter arrived in June from Archbishop Dewdney complaining about the noise.

While hosting groups of boys, work continued and the improvements were insured. Club members had invested a lot of sweat equity and were looking forward to use of the camp for a long time. How downcast everyone must have been when, on February 16, 1924, news spread that the Rotary hut and related structures had burned down. The day after the fire, the Boys' Work Committee met at the charred camp and decided to build again.

Reuban Ward recommended that a house be hauled onto the property, where a caretaker could live. Work started on a new Rotary hut. Some in the club wondered about putting permanent structures on leased property, but the membership was in favour.

On Victoria Day, 1924, the club held a celebration at the camp. It was open to the public with the club supplying transportation. "Athletic and carnival events and stunts" took place. The goal was to give some boys and

KANGAROOS

The Rotary Club of Calgary's favourite stories tend to condense over time into jokes. A story of Rotary donating kangaroos to the city has turned into: "Rotary gave the Calgary Zoo a couple of kangaroos in 1916. One bit a Rotarian and died."

Behind the anecdote stands a complicated story. The 1916 part of the anecdote is unlikely, because no zoo existed at St. George's Island then. In 1917, there was a teahouse on the island and a pair of mule deer.

Rotary's involvement in a gift of kangaroos is first mentioned in 1921. It was recorded that member Ernie Willis would soon arrive in Vancouver with two kangaroos, donated by his brother in Australia. Ernie ran the Lyric Theatre and was an early member of the Rotary Club.

For a time, the animals stayed in Vancouver, cared for by that city's Parks Department. They arrived in Calgary in April 1922 and were put in the City's stables, pending transfer to St. George's Island.

That one of the kangaroos died is suggested by the fact that, in early January 1923, Ernie Willis was planning to "taxidermatize" a kangaroo, which he wanted to donate to the city's museum.

The club investigated the purchase of another female kangaroo from Australia but lost interest when they found out it would cost $186. Then came news that the Vancouver Parks Board was willing to part with one at no cost. Whether the zoo's modern day kangaroos are descendants, one does not know, but let's say they are.

girls a good time and to raise money for the camp. But the day also served to plant the idea in parents' minds that this was a good supervised activity for children.

A caretaking couple was found: Mr. and Mrs. Sellers, who would work the four summer months for their rent. The remaining eight months, they would be paid $25 per month. In late summer, a load of winter wood was delivered.

Having again invested in the site, the club was trying hard to negotiate a new agreement. The club wanted a five-year lease rather than three but was also trying to buy the land. The expiration of the lease came and went. The following summer, the club was still without a settlement. The negotiators were hoping for an agreement on the amount they would be paid for improvements if the land were sold from under them.

In the summer of 1926, Archbishop Dewdney complained again, this time about shooting at the camp. A vigorous attempt was made to convince him that the boys were prohibited from having guns. Strictness at the camp went beyond rules about weaponry. A request regarding Sunday-night dancing was voted down and the decision taken that dancing at the camp should be strictly prohibited.

In the summer of 1925, thirteen hundred young people enjoyed stays at the Rotary campground. The following summer, seventeen hundred young people camped there. Even though the camp was successful, the club made up its mind to move it at the end of 1927. Having no lease meant too much uncertainty, and the club asked members J. W. Carlyle, Reuban Ward, and John Hanna to investigate other sites.

It was Carlyle who alerted the board that the federal government had promising land on the Elbow River upstream. In the end, the government wanted only $11 per year for the lease.

By summer 1928, the move to the new camp was well under way. The club sold the old caretakers' house and built a new one. They moved the Rotary hut to the new site. The property needed everything: clearing, surveying, fencing, and road improvements. Lighting and telephone were debated, and, in the meantime, Matt Brownlee loaned the camp his Delco light plant. Club members again did much of the work, and J. W. Carlyle and George Hughes were singled out for thanks.

The new campground was not far from the old Sam Livingston house. Livingston, an Irishman who participated in the California gold rush of 1849, is sometimes described as "Calgary's first citizen." He was related through marriage to the pioneer Edworthy family (which has produced three generations of Calgary Rotarians). Livingston's Elbow Valley farm was named "Glenmore," Gaelic for "big valley."

Glenmore was also the name chosen by the City of Calgary for its new water reservoir. The sad news was that Rotary's campground would soon be under water.

It is difficult to tell from club documents exactly when the club knew its latest camp was doomed. The March 31, 1930, board minutes state: "Report received on our claim against the city in expropriation of the Rotary camp site. Claim lodged at $15, 480.17." Also that day, it is mentioned that the YWCA wanted to book the camp for part of the coming summer. "Instructed to advise them of the present condition of affairs at the camp."

It is interesting that, just two weeks later, J. S. McMurchy appeared at a Rotary board meeting on behalf of the YMCA to outline plans for a new camp at "Beaufort Falls." They had a forty-nine-year lease on sixty acres of the Stoney Indian Reserve and planned to spend $10,000 on a main building and ten huts for boys to sleep in.

IN THE 1920S, the club created campgrounds where city boys could play in a natural environment.

McMurchy was asking the Rotary Club to fund the construction of the main building: "a free gift from the club entailing no further obligation." When The Rotary Club of Calgary finally received a cheque for $12,256.17 from the City of Calgary for expropriation of its campground, it plunged into construction at Bow Fort.

Over time, the name for the new YMCA camp kept changing in the Rotary Club's records. It went from "Beaufort," to "Bow Fort," and, in July 1931, became "Camp Chief Hector" (after Stoney Chief Hector Crawler). Beaufort was no more than a typo, but Bow Fort referred to a Hudson's Bay Company fort that had existed nearby in the 1830s.

When the club's work at Camp Chief Hector was finished, Cecil Brown conveyed the YMCA's thanks. Brown expressed the opinion that it was "the best investment Calgary Rotary had ever made."

On June 27, 1931, the official opening of Camp Chief Hector was marked by a picnic. Presidents of the local service clubs were invited. Ice cream, homemade lemonade, and peanuts were provided courtesy of Rotary.

Calgary's Rotary Club had less connection with Camp Chief Hector after it opened, but many individual Rotarians continued to pay to send underprivileged young people there.

One more footnote to the Camp Chief Hector story: for those people who may be scratching their heads at the above location, Camp Chief Hector's present location is not the same as the one where the camp began. In 1972, the Stoney Nation took over the old camp and renamed it Nakoda Lodge. Keeping the name Camp Chief Hector, the YMCA moved south of the Trans-Canada Highway to Chilver Lake, its present location.

• • •

AFTER CAMP CHIEF HECTOR, The Rotary Club of Calgary moved on to an infrastructure project closer to home: the building of a city playground. Because of the onset of the Great Depression, the City could not afford new playgrounds, and the club stepped in.

The club was also acting in response to an RI directive. In 1931, RI sent out a letter to all clubs recommending the building and equipping of playgrounds as a good form of community service. A month after that circular, a committee of Nat Christie, Jim Quigley, Charlie Hayden, and Bill Osborne began considering a playground on Calgary's North Hill. Ernie Richardson was committee chair.

The depression slowed things to such a degree that, two years later, the club had still not completed the North Hill playground. Ernie Richardson informed the club that $1,500 more was needed to finish.

THE EDWORTHY ROTARIANS

The Rotary Club of Calgary is known for family acts: families in which more than one generation has held membership. The Jenkins family and the Morrison family are two examples.

Currently, the Edworthy family has the bragging rights. George E. Edworthy joined the club in 1942 and was a prominent member for decades. His son, Calgary optometrist Dr. George H. Edworthy, is still a member. Dr. Edworthy's sons Jason and Dr. Gene Edworthy are also current members of the club.

Dr. George Edworthy has given a few Calgary history reviews at club luncheons, usually in cowboy garb, commencing with a hollered, "Yahoo!" His grandfather, Tom Edworthy, was a rancher on the south banks of the Bow River beginning in 1883. Part of that ranch is now Calgary's Edworthy Park and contains the old Edworthy ranch house. Tom Edworthy married Mary Ross, the widow of photographer Alex Ross. Mary Edworthy's side of the family is related to pioneer farmer and rancher Sam Livingston, part of whose farm is now the bottom of Calgary's Glenbow Reservoir. Glenbow was the name Sam Livingston gave to his farm.

The Edworthy family is one of very few that can claim to have been in Calgary before the coming of the railroad.

(TOP LEFT) **MARY AND TOM EDWORTHY** (ca. 1895). The Edworthy family arrived in Calgary before the railroad. (ABOVE) **GEORGE E. EDWORTHY,** son of Tom Edworthy, joined The Rotary Club of Calgary in 1942. (BOTTOM LEFT) **GEORGE EDWORTHY** (son of George E.) with his sons Gene (L) and Jason (R) are current members of The Rotary Club of Calgary.

It was 1936 before the final work was done. But, by that summer, the club was ready for more. It committed to two more playgrounds: 16th Avenue and 11th Street NW, and 12th Avenue and 6th Street SE.

There was an assumption that, when the club built playgrounds, the City would take them over and look after them. This seems to have been clearer to Rotary than to the City. When the club investigated the North Hill recreation ground in the summer of 1936, it found the toilets in sad shape. Vandalism was another problem, and to protect the parks and make them available after dark, the club built more fences and put up lighting.

Further vandalism, in 1937 at Rotary's 16th Avenue and 11th Street park, brought things to a head. Rotary sent another letter to the city commissioners, and made it clear that the club's undertaking more playground building depended on the reply. Another concern was liability. If the City had not truly taken over responsibility for the parks, was Rotary liable for accidents?

All the same, the club went ahead with more playgrounds. They had ordered equipment for one in Bankview and began discussing yet another near City Hall. The final playground in this plan was across from the Calgary Brewery on 9th Avenue E: a triangular plot between roads.

The argument with the City over responsibility for playgrounds continued. Vandalism, disrepair, and rowdiness at club-built parks did not add to Rotary's reputation the way the building and donation of parks should have done. Letters passed back and forth. A definite change of tone came in 1941. The City clerk sent a letter thanking The Rotary Club of Calgary for all the playground work it had done.

Late in the depression, the club branched into other kinds of construction. In the summer of 1938, it built a solarium for the Junior Red Cross Hospital for Crippled Children (the former Raby/Laurendeau house on Royal Avenue in Mount Royal). This having gone well, they followed in 1939 with a sunroom at an old folks' home.

• • •

AN AMAZING THING about the club's infrastructure-building days is the responsibility it felt for everything it did. Instead of giving up on campgrounds after the Rotary hut fire of 1924, the club rebuilt. When it had to move, it moved. When the second camp was expropriated, the club still felt it should do something for the young in need of a place to camp and so contributed the main building to the original Camp Chief Hector.

Likewise, when it came to playgrounds, it did not simply build them, give them to the city, pat itself on the back, and walk away; it inspected the parks. Often, the club paid for repairs.

Perhaps the best example of continuity came in 1958. The YMCA got in touch with the club to say that, though the main lodge at Camp Chief Hector (built in 1931) was still in good shape, the kitchen needed a rebuild.

Some within the club argued over whether rebuilding the YMCA's campground kitchen was a good investment. The argument in favour was that it would serve to remind the membership that, twenty-six years ago, the original building had been erected by The Rotary Club of Calgary and given to the YMCA. That argument won the day, and Harry Hays's board unanimously approved the cost of the kitchen's reconstruction.

Citizens OF Tomorrow

3

THE MOST CONSISTENT FOCUS of The Rotary Club of Calgary over its first one hundred years has been youth: campgrounds, playgrounds, Christmas parties, children's hospitals, Boys' and Girls' Clubs, Boys' Work Committees, youth leadership, student exchanges, scholarships, and life enrichment. The simplest answer for why this is so is that a service club, run by service-oriented people, seeks to help society's most vulnerable: the suffering, the elderly, and the young.

WOOD'S HOMES AND DR. "MAC" MCINTYRE

Wood's Homes (known as Wood's Christian Homes until 2007) began as an orphanage in 1914, the same year The Rotary Club of Calgary was born. The story of its origin was that a soldier had come up to Presbyterian Minister George Wood on the streets of Innisfail in 1914 to ask the minister to look after his two motherless children while he fought overseas. Rev. Wood agreed; the soldier died in the war. Wood's Christian Homes went on to become a prominent non-profit orphanage in Calgary.

Calgary dentist Dr. Raeburn "Mac" McIntyre did free dental work for children at Wood's Homes during the Great Depression. Known for his charity, Dr. McIntyre was also an avid hunter of birds. He supplied birds to at least one Rotary fowl dinner. Calgary's Rotary Club backed Dr. McIntyre's dental work at Wood's Homes by covering the cost of supplies.

Wood's Homes continues in Calgary to this day, providing a wide spectrum of services to vulnerable children and families all over Alberta.

THE BOYS' DORMITORY OF WOOD'S CHRISTIAN HOMES in Bowness, 1931. During the Great Depression, Dr. Raeburn "Mac" McIntyre did free dental work at Wood's Christian Homes, and The Rotary Club of Calgary paid for his supplies.

WHEN CALGARY'S ROTARY CLUB was newly chartered and looking for projects, Rotary's head office was concerned about juvenile delinquency and suggested the Calgary club start programs for problem boys. Rotary International was advising its clubs to set up Boys' Work Committees, "Boys' Work" being the term governments both in the U.S. and Canada were using.

By the time the International Association of Rotary Clubs held its ninth convention in Kansas City in 1918, 155 Rotary Clubs had Boys' Work Committees, but many remained at sea as to what activities they should sponsor. At the conference, C. J. Atkinson of New York, chairman of the Committee for Work Among Boys, suggested club members determine what boys' lives were like in their city. How many were under eighteen? What percentage turned up in court and went to reformatories?

The goal of Boys' Work, Mr. Atkinson said, was to help boys develop into good citizens. By studying the situation in its home city, a Boys' Work Committee ought to be able to come up with a list of problems. Find the top problem not already dealt with and take it on.

The glaring problem for many boys in Calgary in the war years, 1914–18, was their fathers being away. As the long and terrible war raged on, many boys and girls lost their fathers forever. Another problem, described by Edmonton Rotarian Sam Dickson, was that many boys lied about their age to get into the army. By the time they were found out and sent back to the streets, they "drifted into lines where they weren't getting the best out of life."

In 1919–20, during James Wheeler Davidson's presidency, Calgary's Rotary Club initiated its first Boys' Work projects. Rev. Bob Pearson was the chairman of the Boys' Work Committee at the time. In 1921, eighty-five boys were invited to a Tuesday luncheon, and Dr. Lincoln

In 1927, Rotary International announced that 160 Australian boys were on a world tour, and Rotary Clubs were hosting them. Would Calgary like to be involved? Cecil Brown was put in charge, and he asked W. W. Grant of CFCN Radio to broadcast the visit. Frank Freeze wrote to Alberta's Premier Brownlee to see if the Province would pay for a dinner at the Palliser. The Australian boys were popular visitors, and, after they left, telegrams of farewell were sent to Vancouver, to reach them before they took ship for home.

and John Hanna combined on a forcible talk about the necessity of education.

In these early days, Calgary's Rotary Club was still deciding where its funds and service should go. What was the club's business and what was not? When it came to young people, the club felt boys were their business more than girls. The guidance of girls was better left to women.

In 1922, the Boys' Work Board of Alberta asked for funds, and the club complied. That same year, the club made a contribution to the YMCA for a camp for under-privileged boys. When the Girls' Work Board of Alberta asked for funds, the club said the request was "beyond their scope." In 1923, the club also turned down a request from Daughters of the Empire to support a summer camp for girls.

But it wasn't quite a boys-only rule. In 1925, the board voted to pay entrance exam fees for four girls trying to complete grade twelve. The club continued to help with exam fees while lobbying the provincial government to remove this obstacle to the education of underprivileged youth.

In the 1920s, Rotary International encouraged clubs to engage Dr. Charles E. Barker to come to their city. A Doctor of Hygiene and Physical Culture, Dr. Barker had been health advisor to U.S. President Taft. Dr. Barker addressed the International Conference of Rotary Clubs in Salt Lake City in 1919, and many who heard him wanted to book the dynamic speaker for their home clubs. In 1920, Rotary International took Dr. Barker on full-time as a touring ambassador.

Calgary's Rotary Club booked Dr. Barker in 1923 and again in 1926. Though we have no record of how the local club or the recipients of the lectures responded to Dr. Barker, his topics give a good summary of Rotary's concerns when it came to youth. To high schools, he delivered "How to Get the Most Out of Life." To women's meetings, his speech was "A Mother's Relation to Her Daughter." At men's meetings: "A Father's Responsibility to His Son."

● ● ●

THE ROTARY CLUB OF CALGARY often teamed with other organizations on behalf of the young. In 1926, when Charlie Baker chaired the Boys' Work Committee, he informed the board that the YMCA had started a Boys' Club in Riverside. The Y needed money to fix up the Riverside fire hall as the club's permanent home.

The idea of a Boys' Club goes all the way back to 1860, when the name was first used in New Haven, Connecticut, to refer to a reading room and coffee shop for street youth. The Canadian story started in St. John, New Brunswick, in 1900, when the local citizenry began a public playgrounds movement so homeless youths would have a place to go after school. In winter, those boys were guided to what is now recognized as Canada's first Boys' Club. These efforts tended to centre on boys who were orphaned or otherwise did not have parental guidance. Boys rather than girls were chosen because it was thought, perhaps naively, that boys were at more risk.

In Calgary in 1926, Rotarians Reuban Ward, John Bell, and Jack Stanley interviewed Calgary's mayor about the status of the Riverside fire hall and gave a favourable report. The club paid for the conversion of the old fire hall into a Boys' Club, and the opening celebration took place in June that year. Rotary's J. W. Carlyle was thanked for his leadership.

Through the depression, Calgary's Rotary Club maintained its interest in the Riverside Boys' Club. In 1939, when the YMCA alerted Rotary to the need for a Boys' Club downtown, the club found basement rooms in J. Singer's Carlton Hotel on 9th Avenue, not far from the YMCA. Mr. Singer provided the premises rent-free for a year.

Club representatives were invited to view the Boys' Club's downtown rooms in 1940, and the visit proved pivotal. The infrastructure-building phase of the club's early life was winding down, and so was the financial stringency of the depression. The club was looking for its next major commitment, and the tour of the downtown Boys' Club suggested this could be it. While continuing to partner with the Y on Riverside Boys' Club, the club wanted to take over solo control of the downtown Boys' Club.

The club's adoption of the downtown Boys' Club (which they called "Boys' Town") started as World War II broke out. This gave Boys' Club an even greater purpose, as once again many boys would be doing without their fathers. Boys' Town was a place where they could go to play sports, learn skills, and stay out of trouble.

Rotary placed Bill Blatchford in charge of its Boys' Town. Blatchford described the situation this way:

> The City of Calgary has, like many cities, a boys' problem. This problem exists mainly in the downtown area, where living conditions are poor and housing accommodation is over-crowded. In this area, no provision has been made for recreation facilities for the children living in over-crowded blocks and tenements. A few years ago Rotary undertook to equip a playground in the heart of this area on a piece of ground set aside by the city. The usual equipment was installed and this proved to be a great relief, as it provides a playground for many under-privileged children. This did not, however, meet the boy problem, as most of the boys were too old to spend their time in a playground . . . and were accustomed during out of school hours to be on the streets and in the alleys, and caused the police no end of worry.

Boys' Town continued in the basement of the Carlton Hotel for many years. Boys between nine and seventeen registered as club members. The club was open to them from seven to ten every evening. The facilities consisted of a library and a manual training room, complete with automobile engine, lathes, and a full set of woodworking tools. In another room were boxing gloves, wrestling mats, punching bags, and dumbbells.

Police constables attended most nights, helping the boys construct model airplanes and pieces of furniture. Rotary tried to have at least one member visit each evening. A long lineup of boys waited to get in every night, and it was difficult to get them to go home. They never left until the place was properly cleaned and the floor scrubbed. Boys' Club members were also allowed into the YMCA pool for a free swim once a week.

Each summer, Rotary Club members sent as many as eighty of the boys from Boys' Town to the YMCA's Camp Chief Hector. One summer, the Rotary Boys' Town baseball team was so good it made the provincial finals. Rotary members saw that the boys got to Edmonton to contest the final tournament.

The underlying purpose of Boys' Town was to keep the boys out of trouble, and the results were positive. When the downtown club opened, fifty-six of its members had records in juvenile court. During the club's first winter, only eight members made court appearances.

What Boys' Town lacked was space. The basement rooms under the Carlton were also cold and poorly ventilated. Several times during the war, the Rotary Club applied for a permit to construct a new building for its Boys' Club, and each time it was rejected by the wartime controller. A short-term solution was found in 1943 when the Rotary Club was able to acquire the old Ukrainian Hall on 7th Avenue SE. But the goal of a new building remained.

(TOP) **THE WOOD-WORKING SHOP** at Calgary's Boys' Town. The Rotary Club's goal was to have at least one member at Boys' Town every night. (BOTTOM) **CALGARY'S ROTARY CLUB** became involved with Boys' Club in 1926. It was the sole supporter of the downtown Boys' Town from 1940 to 1952 and continued to give project funding to Calgary's Boys' and Girls' Clubs long after that.

IN 1975, BOYS' CLUBS OF CALGARY changed its name to Boys & Girls Clubs of Calgary. Calgary's first Rotary Club supported the organization from the 1920s through the 1950s, and it is still going strong.

In May 1949, the relationship between Calgary's Rotary Club and the Rotary Boys' Club fundamentally changed. Rotary voted to set up its downtown Boys' Club as a separate organization: an independent institution with the Rotary Club guaranteeing funds for its continuance. To help the Boys' Club along its independent path, Rotary transferred more than $56,000 it had been holding in trust for a new building.

After Boys' Town was under its own management, it remained a favourite cause for Calgary's Rotarians. In 1951–52, club President Harold Morkill summed up the relationship this way: "Boys' Town is now a separate entity from the club, but we feel it is our duty to give it our unqualified support. Its board is headed by Rotarian Glen Elder."

Every year from the end of the war to 1965, The Rotary Club of Calgary gave Boys' Club a donation. In 1965, Rotary informed Boys' Club that it would not, in future, be giving its annual donation, because support from the United Appeal (formerly Community Chest) plus Boys' Club's own fundraising should be enough.

One of the morals of the Boys' Town story is the faithfulness of The Rotary Club of Calgary to its projects. As with its campground initiatives in the twenties and its playground-building of the thirties, Rotary supported Boys' Club year by year until it was fully self-sufficient, a relationship that lasted more than thirty years.

• • •

DURING THE BOYS' CLUB YEARS, a quiet change occurred in the pattern of The Rotary Club of Calgary's support for youth. Rather than focus exclusively on underprivileged boys, the club started to support the education and enrichment of the lives of all young people, regardless of means and gender. The first such move came in Charlie Kennedy's presidential year of 1952–53, when the club sent two Calgary students to "Adventures in Citizenship" in Ottawa, a Rotary Club of Ottawa initiative that allowed students to closely observe the workings of the federal government. This became an annual project.

When The Rotary Foundation began funding scholarships for study abroad in 1947 — travelling scholars acting as peace ambassadors — the Rotary District to which Calgary's club belonged began submitting nominees. In 1963, Rotary Club of Calgary nominee Guy Doll won a Rotary Foundation scholarship and went to the University of Poitiers in France to study. In 1969, Calgarian Margaret Tebbutt used her Rotary Foundation scholarship to study in Montpelier.

World War II and the post-war years brought a new cultural emphasis on the teenage years. Many cultural observers have said the teenager was a 1940s American invention. The explosion of youth-focused popular culture absorbed much of the time and attention of the young, often at the expense of schooling and other more traditional pursuits. Rotary's response was to provide opportunities for people in their teens and twenties to gain a broader experience of community, society, and the world beyond.

To supplement youth scholarships and youth exchange, RI began to introduce youth programs that provided ways for young people to step out of the dominant youth culture, from time to time, and experience the larger society.

The first of these projects was Rotaract, targeted at university students between seventeen and twenty-five. The idea was that a Rotary Club would help start and then guide a Rotaract Club, usually at a college or university, which would take action for positive change. The Rotary Club of Calgary fostered a Rotaract Club at the University of Calgary in the 1970s, which fundraised for several worthy international projects.

The next project in the series was Interact, a similar concept to Rotaract but aimed at a younger age group: junior and senior high school students. The Rotary Club of Calgary chartered an Interact Club at Henry Wise Wood High School in 1975, a co-production with The Rotary Club of South Calgary.

In 1982, when Calgary Rotarian Vinny Jacques was governor of District 536, he announced RI's new District-level youth program called RYLA: Rotary Youth Leadership Awards. RYLA originated in Queensland, Australia, in 1959, when a Rotary Club brought youth leaders to meet Princess Alexandra, Queen Elizabeth II's cousin. By 1970, all Australian and New Zealand Rotary Clubs were participating in youth leadership programs, and Rotary International decided to adopt the concept for the whole of Rotary. At RYLA conferences, Rotary-sponsored student leaders, aged fifteen to eighteen, gather with adult leaders from business, politics, and sport to learn the skills of leadership.

Vinny Jacques asked Rotary Club of Calgary member Bill Kaufmann to organize the District's first RYLA conference. It was to take place in Banff, and Bill Kaufmann and Jack Lamarsh pulled together an impressive crew of mentors: Ken Taylor, Canadian ambassador to Iran during the hostage crisis; national columnist Charles Lynch; Alberta politician Ron Ghitter; energy explorer Jim Gray; and famous Albertan politician and author Grant MacEwan.

The fourth of the new RI youth projects was RYPEN (Rotary Youth Program of Enrichment). It had similarities to RYLA, in that it was a leadership program for youth, but the target group was teenagers between fourteen and seventeen. The other key difference from RYLA was that the invitees had not yet experienced leadership. RYPEN camps use workshops, games — a variety of interactions — to open up the possibilities and rewards of leadership.

Rotaract and Interact clubs, RYLA, and RYPEN gatherings — all of these Rotary youth projects have successfully offered young people bridges into adulthood and leadership; ways of meeting new people, and partaking in real and important societal and international challenges.

● ● ●

THE GOLDEN ANNIVERSARY SCHOLARSHIPS

One of The Rotary Club of Calgary's biggest educational coups came during its fiftieth anniversary year in 1964. The club's Golden Anniversary project was fifty scholarships of $500 for University of Alberta in Calgary students.* All the money was raised from club members.

(FRONT ROW, L TO R:) Maurice Brown, chairman of the Golden Anniversary Committee; Myrl Courtright, president of The Rotary Club of Calgary, 1964–65; Dr. H. S. Armstrong, president of the University of Alberta in Calgary; Holland Cameron, immediate past president of The Rotary Club of Calgary.

IN THIS SAME PERIOD OF TIME, post-1960s, drug and alcohol abuse among the young increased sharply. Calgary Rotarians felt a need to act on the issue.

In February 1988, Dr. Miller Newton, president of KIDS, a New Jersey-based organization dealing aggressively with the addictions of young people, addressed a Rotary Club luncheon at the Palliser Hotel. He explained how his own involvement began with alcohol problems of his teenage son. He received a strong ovation.

The club, under the leadership of President Chuck Simpson, decided to invest in an Alberta facility for dealing with youth drug addiction and contacted Dr. Newton. He responded with a concept called KIDS of the Canadian West.

Since the project would require one of the club's largest-ever outlays, it was thoroughly investigated. Garth Toombs and Dr. Ronald Dougan (an accredited Alberta psychologist) visited KIDS in New Jersey. They found the operation disciplined and well run. KIDS of the Canadian West also offered the club two positions on its board to further guarantee control.

A Calgary club member offered a building as the home of KIDS of the Canadian West. If the provincial and federal governments would contribute half of the appraised amount, the club donor would forgive the rest. In this way, the club's financial commitment was reduced substantially, and it went ahead.

KIDS of the Canadian West will probably go down in club history as its most controversial community

* The University of Alberta opened a branch in Calgary in 1945. The independent University of Calgary was not founded until 1966. That is why the 1964 scholarships were for students bound to UAC (University of Alberta Calgary).

service venture. In February 1990, well before the projected opening date, the *Calgary Herald* ran a series of investigative pieces on the American KIDS operation. It was a negative portrayal. At the heart of the controversy were the tactics used to break young people of their drug addictions. The aggressive approach had led to lawsuits in the U.S.

Expert advisors convinced the club to choose another way of addressing the drug addiction problem. Dr. Ronald Dougan sat on a committee that chose Dr. Dean Vause as executive director of a new organization: the Alberta Adolescent Recovery Centre, or AARC, based on a different approach to drug addiction among the young. Under Dr. Vause's direction AARC has continued operating to this day. In May 2013, AARC celebrated the graduation of its five-hundredth adolescent and family.

● ● ●

ANOTHER YOUTH PROBLEM of the late twentieth century, all across Canada, was school dropouts. In 1991, Canada's federal government organized a round table to investigate how volunteers could supplement its Stay-in-School (SIS) program. Two Calgary Rotarians, Curly Galbraith and Don Campbell, attended, and Curly offered to organize Canada's Rotary Clubs to back the initiative. Under Curly Galbraith's plan, each Rotary Club would come up with its own program. Don Campbell became national chairman of the program in 1992.

Lowell Frodsham asked Calgary's school systems what schools could most use its help. Valleyview and Holy Cross were recommended. At these schools, Rotary organized tours of businesses and museums for the students. Rotarians went into the two schools to read to

CARL SMITH and Stay-in-School students, May 2003.

students. Stay-in-School has always had this hands-on relationship at its core: individual Rotarians working with individual students. In 1994, a third school, Blessed Damien, was added to the club's SIS program.

SIS got a boost when Carl Smith became involved. In addition to the mentoring given by Rotarians to the students, he envisioned adding scholarships. Carl was a retired banker. Back when he was sixteen in Ontario, he'd been a high school dropout. He worked on his father's farm north of Toronto until his father saw an ad for a clerk-trainee at the Dominion Bank. Thirty-eight years later, Carl retired as TD Bank's western regional manager.

Carl's having been a dropout made Stay-in-School "click with him." He had a soft spot for kids who did not go smoothly through youth into post-secondary education. He was living proof there were other paths. He also believed that financial considerations held back many and that a financial incentive would be a critical motivation.

Between 1991 and 1993, when Carl was a Rotary Club of Calgary board member, he found an anonymous donor willing to put up money for the scholarship plan. The donor put up $75,000 and the Rotary Club pledged $50,000, enough to run the program for five years.

The scholarship program's target group was neither top nor bottom students but ones in between: students who principals and teachers identified as financially in need and with potential to finish high school. The children were selected in grade six. They were supported throughout their school years, and, when they left high school, their remaining funds could only be drawn upon if they enrolled in post-secondary education. This was never restricted to academic educations but also included technical and college programs.

The scholarship program began in 1994 with Carl Smith as its chair. Besides seeking donors and sponsors, he stayed in touch with students and their families. If a student hit a snag, Carl tried to figure out the problem. "If they needed a computer, I'd tell them: I'll get you one." He and another man refurbished used computers in Carl's home. Later, he found government programs to supply the computers he needed.

The scholarship stories are often touching. In rare instances, they have been tragic. One student in

AT THE ROOT OF THE ROTARY CLUB OF CALGARY'S STAY-IN-SCHOOL PROGRAM is mentorship: club members like Rotary Partner Maggie Redmond giving one-on-one help to Calgary students.

the program, a young woman, died violently. Another attempted suicide but rallied and was able to enroll in college with Stay-in-School's help.

The tragic death in the program stimulated Rotary to work with Discovery House — a shelter for young women who have suffered abuse — to open an educational path for them. As of 2014, two scholarships are in the works.

As the program grew, so did the need for funding. In the early years, Dennis O'Neil came to Carl Smith and said he was going to put on a golf tournament to raise money for scholarships. He did so almost singlehandedly. Dennis had proven the viability of a charity golf tournament, and Carl Smith sought a sponsor for the next one. Peter McKeen, a Rotarian who ran Jack Carter Chev-Olds in Calgary, convinced Jack Carter of the worthiness of the cause. This has proven one of the strongest and longest lasting of the club's partnerships.

Every year from 1996–97 to the present, the Jack Carter Chev-Olds/Rotary Charity Golf Tournament has produced a stream of money for the Stay-in-School Awards Program. Jack Carter and Peter McKeen were both made Paul Harris Fellows in thanks. John Rockley ran the tournament for many years.

Carl Smith acknowledges many others who have helped with this program. Hank Popoff put years into it, and Joe Fras and Rick Erven worked hard in support of the golf tournament. Rotarian mentors have continued assisting the students. Two more schools have been added to the SIS program, for a total of five. The Rotary Club of Calgary is also one of the partners in the Rotary Tom Jackson Stay-in-School Program. RTJSIS has many similarities to The Rotary Club of Calgary SIS program but is focused on the success of Aboriginal students.

Carl Smith loves to tell stories of the awards

EVER SINCE 1997, the Jack Carter Chev-Olds/Rotary Golf Tournament has raised funds to support The Rotary Club of Calgary's Stay-in-School scholarship program.

program's graduates. One of the first three, Loretta, was confused after finishing high school. She did not know where to go from there. Carl talked to her on the phone, and when she said she "liked wood," he said she should get in touch with the Southern Alberta Institute of Technology and see what they had. She enrolled in cabinet making, stalled for a while, but then returned and won first prize in a class competition. She was proud of this prize and went from success to success after that. "I make good furniture," she says, fully aware of how much her Rotary financial award has helped her.

An extraordinary thing about this long summary of The Rotary Club of Calgary's involvements with young people is that it is not complete. A book of its own would be needed to cover all that has been done for youth in the club's first hundred years. The club has consistently believed, and acted upon the belief, that service to youth is an investment in the future.

A Great Service

James Wheeler Davidson and Douglas Howland

4

THE GOAL OF THE ROTARY MOVEMENT has been to gird the world with an interconnection of clubs; to accomplish through friendship and service what could not always, or even often, be done by politics and force. The goals of Rotary and the state are somewhat the same — peace, harmony, prosperity — but Rotary goes about it by making friends and never carries either a carrot or a stick.

TO EXTEND AROUND THE WORLD means having clubs in every nation and region. Once there are a few, they can extend amongst themselves and become many. The seed clubs, the first in any region, are the key, and it takes a very special kind of human to be effective at frontier extension — especially when the diplomacy is done across cultures and languages.

One of The Rotary Club of Calgary's utmost distinctions is that two of the Rotary movement's greatest extenders were Calgary members: James Wheeler Davidson and Doug Howland. When Paul Harris was asked near the end of his life to name the Rotarians who had made the greatest contributions, he named James Wheeler Davidson as one.

JAMES WHEELER DAVIDSON had many involvements with the city of Calgary. In 1912, he had a hand in commissioning Thomas Mawson to design a new vision for Calgary's downtown: lagoons, fountains, and causeways in the Eau Claire-Prince's Island vicinity. Due to World War I, the Mawson Plan did not advance beyond the drawing stage.

JAMES W. DAVIDSON'S LIFE (1872–1933) was full of legend: rare adventures, great risks taken, near escapes, fascinating interests, life-changing consequences, accomplishments, sudden changes in direction both forced and chosen, and, everywhere he went, friends made. His biography reads like a hair-raising fiction or like the lives of several great men welded into one.

In terms of The Rotary Club of Calgary, the legend of Jim Davidson begins with his being an indifferent Rotarian during his first years in the club. He was not a founding member of the Calgary club but was led into membership in the first year, 1914, by his friend Jeff Lydiatt. The two were on the first board of the Calgary Symphony and shared a love of performance and show-manship. If Jeff Lydiatt wanted Jim to be a Rotarian, Jim felt he should do so, but for a time his heart was not in it. In those days, Rotary had scant patience for non-attendance, and Jim Davidson might well have been kicked out of the club had Jeff Lydiatt not been on the board to counsel leniency. What an irony if the club's greatest Rotarian had been booted out before he got a chance to prove his mettle.

After three years of poor membership, Jim Davidson's interest kicked in. He became the Calgary Rotary Club's president in 1919–20 and, from there onward, was a Rotarian through and through.

To understand James W. Davidson's contribution to Rotary's worldwide extension between 1921 and 1931, one has to go back to his early life. He was born in Austin, Minnesota, and was educated in the Northwestern Military Academy. At eighteen, he organized tours for his hometown opera house and came to the attention of

JEFF LYDIATT, pictured here, kept Davidson in The Rotary Club of Calgary — despite his poor attendance record — long enough to become one of the club's greatest Rotarians.

his cousin, Major Pond, one of the most powerful theatre impresarios of his era. Major Pond hired young Jim to organize American tours for VIPs, a group that included the famous explorers Henry Stanley and Lt. Robert Peary.

ASSEMBLY AT THE 1989 ROTARY INTERNATIONAL CONFERENCE at Phoenix, Arizona: a powerful illustration of the worldwide extension of the Rotary movement.

In 1893, Jim Davidson was one of eight men selected out of fifteen hundred applicants for the second Peary Expedition. The purpose of the expedition was to seek a way across the Greenland Ice Cap to the North Pole. Forty-five miles from the expedition's Greenland base camp, Peary's team was stopped by an extreme seven-day storm. Of the two tents, the one in which Jim sheltered was torn to pieces by the storm, and, in the course of digging out his companions and making the move to Peary's larger tent, Davidson's sleeping bag became wet. As the storm continued, his feet froze solid. There was no hope of his continuing, as he could not walk. The expedition surgeon, Dr. Vincent — with one sled, four half-starved dogs, and a few supplies — attempted to take Davidson back. Both men came close to dying. A skin graft from an Inuit boy saved Davidson's feet, but he would walk with a limp for the rest of his life.

Of this experience, Davidson said: "The young man who once participates in such an expedition is rarely content with any other vocation upon his return. Arctic exploration can scarcely be called a profession and thus the careers of many promising young men are injured rather than advanced." In this statement may reside the secret of why James Wheeler Davidson was so ready to drop everything and travel in the cause of Rotary.

The second Peary Expedition failed to find the North Pole. A Newfoundland relief ship brought the crew south, and, while on board, Jim made a friend of a New York journalist. From this newsman, he learned of the Chinese Qing Dynasty's war with Meiji Japan and conceived a powerful wish to go to China as a correspondent. In 1895, he did so, representing several newspapers.

When a truce in the Sino-Japanese war was signed but did not include Formosa (Taiwan), Davidson knew it meant catastrophe for the island. He went there immediately. The Japanese quickly invaded Formosa, and the Chinese governor escaped, causing unpaid Chinese soldiers to begin rioting and setting fires in the city of Taipei. Having been with the Chinese, Davidson now crossed lines to the Japanese side, where he convinced the Japanese commander to assign an army to occupy Taipei. This non-violent action saved the city and its population from further destruction. James Wheeler Davidson was awarded Japan's Order of the Rising Sun, and the people of Formosa never forgot him.

The United States Government understood that Jim Davidson had a talent for diplomacy. In 1896, he was offered the post of U.S. Consul Agent in Formosa. While there, he wrote a book about the island, past and present, which is still admired. After Formosa came diplomatic postings to Manchuria and Shanghai. For six months of 1903, he was on loan to Russia, writing articles about the Trans-Siberian Railway.

What ended this period of Davidson's life was typhoid. Suffering from the disease, he returned by ship to San Francisco in 1905. On board, he met the Dow family of San Francisco and his soon-to-be wife, Lillian Dow. In 1906, James Wheeler Davidson and Lillian Dow were married.

The couple moved to Winnipeg in 1906, where Jim's brother Charles was involved in developing land for immigrant farmers. The following year, the Davidsons moved to Calgary to develop two blocks of CPR land northeast and southeast of Calgary. Once there, Jim became president and managing director of Crown Lumber Co. By 1912, the company had fifty-two lumberyards across western Canada.

•　•　•

TWO CANADIAN ROTARIANS, Dr. Crawford McCullough and Jeff Lydiatt, played key roles in encouraging and enabling James W. Davidson to become "the Marco Polo of Rotary." Dr. McCullough of Fort William-Port Arthur became governor of Rotary District 19 in 1919–20, a district stretching from northwestern Ontario to Alberta. While governor, he pushed for a Canadian Advisory Committee in the International Association of Rotary Clubs (IARC). Jeff Lydiatt was chosen to chair that committee in 1920–21, the year McCullough ascended to first vice-president of IARC.

At the time, IARC badly wanted to extend Rotary into Australia and New Zealand. Crawford McCullough, being Canadian and understanding the connections between Dominions of the former British Empire, suggested Canadian Rotarians do the job. He put the Canadian Advisory Committee, chaired by Lydiatt, in charge of choosing a team. Quite naturally, Lydiatt's first choice was James Wheeler Davidson.

The other half of the extension team was Lt. Col. James Layton Ralston, former president of the Halifax Rotary Club and a decorated hero in World War I. Ralston would later become Canada's Minister of Defence.

Ralston and Davidson agreed to take a year off from their businesses. They set out for Australia in the company of their wives in 1921. The campaign began in Melbourne, proceeded to Sydney, and then crossed the Tasman Sea to New Zealand, where clubs were spawned in Wellington and Auckland. Davidson and Ralston took fourteen days to found each club, and the methods they developed would continue to be Jim Davidson's strategy for the rest of his club-founding career. One key was to meet with each Rotary prospect alone. That way, you could deal with negative ideas and concerns without the negativity spreading to others in the room. Another technique was to start at the top. If they could convince governors and top businessmen, the others would follow.

A funny story coming out of the Australian venture concerned alcohol. Lt. Col. Ralston was a non-drinker, and this sparked a rumour that Rotary was a teetotal organization. This could have been the death of Rotary in Australia had Jim Davidson not pitched in and taken a drink whenever one was offered. In his retellings of the tale, he called it one of the many sufferings he had undergone for the sake of his beloved Rotary. The Antipodean venture was a success, and the four seed clubs soon multiplied.

In the years following Jim Davidson's return to Calgary, he was elected District governor. In his year as governor, he founded five more Rotary Clubs, a District record he shared with Dr. McCullough. The clubs were Camrose, Stettler, Drumheller, and Banff, in Alberta, as well as Dauphin, Manitoba.

In the 1920s, Jim Davidson sat on several RI committees, served as a director, and became, finally, third vice-president. His work on RI's Extension Committee in 1926 and 1927 was critical, for it dealt with the challenge of bringing Asia and the Middle East into Rotary. When Jim joined the Extension Committee, there was still but one Rotary Club between Prague and Shanghai: the venerable Rotary Club of Calcutta. In 1927, the number doubled to two with the chartering of a club in Lahore. Jim Davidson believed strongly that Rotary must do something to rapidly change this weakness in Asia, or the movement would not deserve the International part of its name.

In 1928, Jim was asked to take charge of the problem himself, on an eight-month journey through Asia Minor to the Far East. He was given the title Honorary General Commissioner of Rotary International. The journey began in August 1928 with $8,000 of Rotary International backing. Jim, Lillian, and their daughter Marjory left Montreal on the *Duchess of Athol*.

JIM AND LILLIAN DAVIDSON, and their daughter Marjory, left Canada in 1927: the objective being for Jim to extend Rotary throughout Asia.

The first stage was Europe. There, Jim did not seek to found any clubs but made contacts and collected letters of introduction from politicians, royals, and businessmen whose names would carry weight on the journey ahead. Jim's experience told him that few doors would open unless he could prove he had the confidence of powerful people.

The club-founding portion of the journey began in Greece. Jim gained the support of Greek Prime Minister Venizelos and was able to found a club in Athens. Next, he founded clubs in Cairo and Jerusalem. In Turkey, Syria, Iraq, and Persia, the problems outweighed the potential for success. There was no choice but to move on. At this stage and throughout, Jim used the system he and Lt. Col. Ralston had perfected in 1921: one-hour interviews, starting at the top.

In India, the Davidsons' tour added three more clubs: Bombay, Delhi, and Madras. The family moved on to Ceylon (Sri Lanka), where Jim was again successful in Colombo.

Before Jim had left North America, RI had asked if he would write articles about the journey for *The Rotarian*. Jim told them he would rather stick to club-founding while Lillian wrote the articles. By journey's end, Jim had entertained twenty-two hundred men in their offices, and Lillian's *Rotarian* articles were hugely popular. The articles would eventually be brought together in the book *Making New Friends*.

The obstacles Jim Davidson was maneuvering through can be guessed by the recommendations he made in his final report to RI. Rather than simply list his successes and failures, he strove to explain the culture and value collisions that would require changes on Rotary's part if they were to win over Asia. Just sitting down for a weekly

(TOP) **MARJORY DAVIDSON** has a go at elephant riding in Malay States (Malaysia).
(BOTTOM) **JIM DAVIDSON** interviews a Rotary prospect in Ceylon (Sri Lanka).

lunch was not simple if the members were a mix of religions. Some would eat meat; some would not; some would not eat anything with utensils an infidel had touched.

Rotary's strict attendance rules made no sense in countries where well-off citizens left town in the hot months for a cooler region. The classification system was another problem. Many citizens of Asian cities, who were desirable for Rotary, did not have work as defined in the book of classifications. Some had myriad interests that made a question like, "What is your key area of work?" seem out-of-touch.

One of the clubs Davidson worked with had interpreted the Rotary classification rule — one member per classification — as meaning one person of each ethnic/religious group per classification. Jim Davidson said that, while the Rotarian in him recoiled, he began to see it as fairly sensible given the culture. For example, each lawyer in this club's community had his own community of citizens to draw on, and there was no overlap. All could be members of the same Rotary Club without ever competing.

These kinds of suggestions required fundamental changes in how Rotary did business, but Jim believed Rotary could not succeed in these cultures without bending its own rules in the direction of their values.

Jim's next success was a club in Rangoon, Burma. He went on to succeed in Java, Sumatra, Singapore, the Malay States, and Siam. Between Singapore and Malacca the family was driven by a Malay chauffeur who seemed to be "pursued by furies," as Lillian wrote. Emerging from the jungle, he took a turn too sharply, struck a metal telephone pole, and broke it in half. "The car turned turtle and fortunately dumped us in a muddy ditch." The nearest villagers came quickly. "They unfastened the luggage and took us to a thatched hut where we could get into dry clothes." Another car was found, and they continued to Malacca. Jim and Marjory needed tetanus shots. Lillian had an attack of malaria brought on by the shock. In Lillian's words, "We escaped with little damage."

From Siam (Thailand), the family went overland through Cambodia and into Indo-China, for which Jim had letters of introduction from French officials. Then it was on to Hong Kong, Canton, and the Philippines. The final nations visited were Formosa, Korea, and Japan.

JIM DAVIDSON at a Balinese temple.

The visit to Formosa had great emotional significance for Jim, who had spent nine years of his life there. He was delighted to find that he was still remembered.

While in Japan, Jim collapsed and required a hospital stay. The family returned to Canada by steamer.

The popularity of the Davidsons, the delight at having them back in Canada, made it practically impossible to *get* home. A crowd of people awaited them in Vancouver. On the train through the mountains, they were met in Field, BC, by Mr. Halkett's car. In the car were Rotary friends J. W. Carlyle, Lon Cavanaugh, and Dr. Gunn. At the station in Calgary: another crowd.

The Calgary Rotarians had a dinner in the Davidsons' honour at the Palliser Hotel. Four hundred Rotarians and their wives, plus representatives of other service clubs, turned out. Mayor Andy Davison and District Governor Bruce Richardson gave praise. Long-time Calgary Rotarian Frank Freeze, current chair of the Canadian Advisory Board, analyzed the impact of Jim Davidson extensions. In two and a half years, he had founded thirty-three Rotary Clubs in twelve countries. To commemorate the achievement, the Davidsons were given a sterling silver tray engraved with a map of the trail they had blazed.

In his speech that night, and in many speeches in the months to come, Jim Davidson downplayed his achievement. Of his and Ralston's journey in 1921, he said, "I had to do with organizing the first club in Australia and New Zealand, but I can scarcely be credited with the fact that the Australians have gone ahead and started some thirty other clubs, and that the men of New Zealand have increased the number in that snug land to twenty-four."

Of the recent odyssey, he said, "I feel that I went to Asia at a psychological time. I do not believe that I would have met with equal success five or ten years ago. This fact should be borne in mind when you are inclined to praise my efforts in some of these cities where others, years before, have made efforts to start Rotary Clubs and failed."

But Dr. Crawford McCullough, who had seen it all, praised Jim Davidson's achievement as unique.

He has done a great service. How great will perhaps never be measured . . . Perhaps if Rotary had gone searching the world over, she would never have found the militant apostle that she needed for this work in the near and far east. There are no other fellows . . . like Jim Davidson. His personality is distinctly and entirely his own. It is an odd conglomerate of seer, politician, showman, adventurer, writer-philosopher, incorrigible youth, and go-getter. And it took the whole repertoire to succeed. Indeed, I believe he succeeded where no one else could have.

After the Davidsons return to Calgary, they prepared themselves for a move to Vancouver. This was a blow to Calgary as Jim and Lillian Davidson were much-loved citizens. The Davidsons lived on Royal Avenue on the north face of the Mount Royal hill, a part of town that had the nickname "American Hill," because of the Davidsons and other Americans who had made it their home. Another version of the story credits Jim with bestowing the nickname. Every morning, for years, the Davidsons had a morning open house, where fellow Rotarians were welcome to drop in and have coffee.

Jim was beloved too for his private enthusiasms. Just before the Regent Theatre was demolished to make way for the expansion of the Hudson's Bay Company's downtown store, Jim rescued the theatre's pipe organ and brought it home. While he visited with company, he liked to put on the organ's player piano rolls and manipulate the stops as the conversation went on. He had a boat called the *Atta Girl*, which he greatly enjoyed. Then there was the circus. The showman never lost his love of circuses and never missed one when it came to town. All his life, he'd spent time with circus people, even travelled with them, and that community loved him back. Of this part of his life, Lillian said, "He had great admiration for these men who could take their losses without bitterness and often with the same cheerfulness as their successes . . . When he was with them, he was one of them."

The Davidsons made their move to Vancouver, but Jim's health, damaged by his last great Rotary adventure, never recovered. On July 19, 1933, James Wheeler Davidson died.

At the 1934 Rotary International Convention in Detroit, five thousand delegates stood in a darkened auditorium to hear the RI past president deliver a memorial address to Davidson. People were mourning his death all over the world. When a three-ring circus next visited Vancouver, the crew went to Jim's crypt at Ocean View Cemetery and conducted a ceremony of their own.

● ● ●

AFTER JIM DAVIDSON RETURNED from Asia and the Far East, one of his concerns was that the newly founded clubs not be left to chance; that is, rather than leave them to sink or swim, he hoped they could be visited soon to show support and work on any problems that might have developed. There was a system in Rotary for doing this type of work; it was called "back-tracking." He was asking that someone back-track his journey through Asia.

It seems likely that Jim Davidson chose the man to do this work. When Jim joined Rotary in Calgary in 1914,

THIS PAINTING OF JAMES WHEELER DAVIDSON, with scenes and locations of importance to his life, hangs in the foyer of the Palliser Hotel, just outside the ballroom where so many Rotary Club of Calgary functions and galas have been held. The Rotary Club of Calgary commissioned the painting for Rotary's one-hundredth anniversary in 2005.

the first secretary of the club was Douglas Howland. Doug had done a lot of the contacting and cajoling of people that had brought the Calgary club together. He was a capable writer and had penned some of the earliest accounts of the young club. It seems likely that Jim Davidson admired Doug Howland's style, which was perhaps a little on the formal side of Rotarianism. In his report to RI on his return from Japan, Jim spent quite a bit of time discussing the tradition in some clubs of giving everyone a hilarious nickname. This sort of thing went over big in North America but could be seriously off-putting to those in Asia and elsewhere. Doug Howland, English by birth, was not the type to make that sort of mistake, or any other kind of diplomatic blunder.

This story also involves the Calgary club's executive-secretary, Verena Williams, who everyone called "Jack." Back in 1914, Verena had been married to popular founder-member James Williams. Jim was a wonderful singer, a baritone, who soloed in the club's minstrel show. Jim died suddenly of a ruptured appendix, leaving Verena a young widow with three children. When the Calgary Rotary Club went looking for an executive secretary for their Palliser Hotel office, Verena "Jack" Williams got the job, part-time at first and then full-time. She worked for the club for twenty-five years.

The original members of Calgary's Rotary Club were close. Jim and Verena Williams were a popular couple. Their youngest son, Jefferey, born in 1920, was named after Jeff Lydiatt. When Jim Williams died, Fred Osborne, an early Rotary president, and his wife Flossie were Jack's close friends. In 1933, Jack enrolled her son Jeff in a school where Rotarian Fred Weir taught. He was reputed to be the best Latin and Mathematics teacher in western Canada. When Jeff Williams went to camp, it was the YMCA camp with which Rotarian Rev. Swanny Swanson was affiliated. Jack's world was a Rotary world, and also part of that world was her close friend Doug Howland.

Jack was a farm girl from Ontario, outdoorsy and sporty. She was a good shot and could drive a team of horses. She and Doug Howland were avid golfers who often played at the Calgary Golf and Country Club. Jack's son Jeff remembered going in Doug Howland's Model A to Fish Creek where he was able to swim.

Jeff Williams wrote a memoir called *Far from Home*. He was able to recall the day that Doug Howland left Calgary for Asia because he had never before seen his mother smoke a cigarette. She and Flossie Osborne

had whiskies and cigarettes that night, and it was no celebration.

Doug Howland's journey may have tracked Jim Davidson, but it was also very different. Jim had travelled with his family; Doug travelled alone. Jim Davidson's death came in the middle of Doug's journey, and Lillian's letter to inform him arrived months later. In his response to her, he wrote:

When I reached Batavia [Jakarta], I received over sixty letters and every visit to a new place adds to my official correspondence. I am afraid my friends suffer . . . It seems so terribly hard for me to think that when I get home dear old Jim will not be there to hear all about my trip. Nobody could take as much interest in it as Jim, because I am covering the same ground and could report on the seeds he so ably sowed. So many intimate details that nobody else would appreciate.

● ● ●

DOUG HOWLAND
followed Jim Davidson's trail, consolidating and expanding on Rotary's gains in Asia.

MOUNT DAVIDSON

Eleven kilometres due north of the east end of Lake Minnewanka is a mountain that stands 2,908 metres. It is on the boundary between Banff National Park and Alberta Provincial forestry land. On clear days, its peak can be seen to the right of the black peak called Devil's Head. In 1935, The Rotary Club of Calgary and the Alberta Motor Association, both being clubs beloved of James Wheeler Davidson, worked together to have a mountain named after him, and this was the mountain the Canadian Geographic Names Board chose.

On August 2, 2003, a group of Rotarians and Davidson family members ascended Mount Davidson, in a climb arranged by Red Deer medical doctor and Rotarian Robert Lampard. Dr. Lampard has written extensively about James Wheeler Davidson, and edited the book *The Life and Times of Jim and Lillian Davidson* published by The Rotary Club of Red Deer in 2006. The book brings together many important writings, including Lillian Dow Davidson's essays from *Making New Friends*.

In the end, Doug Howland added fifteen new clubs to Rotary's Asian world: one in Pakistan, six in India, four in China, three in Java, and one in Sumatra. He also followed Jim Davidson's back-trail to Ceylon, Burma, Hong Kong, Malaya, Makassar, and the Philippines.

In his letter to Lillian Davidson from Asia, Doug Howland finished by saying, "The thing I hold dearest in all the world are friends — and they do not live in the East." He returned home to Calgary in 1934. In 1944, he and Verena "Jack" Williams were married. The couple lived their years together in Vancouver, and, when Doug died in 1952, Jack moved back to Calgary, where Rotary had given her so many friends.

In total, the team of James Wheeler Davidson, Lt. Col. Ralston, and Douglas Howland chartered forty-seven clubs in nineteen countries. The numbers are impressive, but the places are even more so: most of them being in countries where Rotary had no traction beforehand. This was truly a Rotary circumnavigation of the planet, leading out from and returning to Calgary.

IN 1943, Lillian Dow Davidson returned to Alberta and spoke to a room full of Rotarians in the Palliser Hotel. She finished her speech with words that should guide all Rotarians:

> You have a wonderful organization in Rotary; an organization founded primarily on friendship, and friendship means understanding and true understanding must be the basis of settlement for all problems. I firmly believe that Rotary in this way can do much in the postwar world to endeavour to ease trying situations that must arise. I think it is the duty of the individual Rotarian and everyone else to try to become more international-minded and to withhold criticism until we inform ourselves. Remember your criticism is only as good as your information.

MR. ROTARY

It was as if George Harshaw "Curly" Galbraith (1921–2010) was born to be a Rotarian. He grew up on a Vulcan area farm, homesteaded by his parents. He went to the Boyne one-room school and later to the school in Vulcan, Alberta. Many decades later, he and his wife went to a small community church one Sunday, and, when Curly was introducing himself to the pastor, a woman piped up from behind that she had been his schoolteacher for several years. The woman was Nan Jensen. Curly had never known until then that his earliest schoolteacher was the niece of Rotary founder, Paul Harris. (Nan Jensen and Martha Cohen joined The Rotary Club of Calgary in 1991 as Honorary Members: the first women in the club.)

Curly went to McGill for his Engineering Degree and to the University of Toronto for a Master's Degree in Business Administration. In his business life, he created and participated in the founding of many companies. He was a community leader and belonged to numerous organizations, but it is probably safe to say that Rotary was his greatest involvement. On that topic, Curly's wife of fifty-five years, Doris Galbraith, says, "I was Curly's second love. The first was Rotary."

Curly joined The Rotary Club of Calgary in 1950. He was involved with almost everything the club did during the time of his membership. He pushed for the club to get into catered barbecues. He organized Canadian Rotary's involvement with the Stay-in-School Program. After being club president in 1970, he moved on to RI, on the Extension and Legislation Committees, and on the board, including as vice-president. In the 1980s, he was on the Legislation Committee that was to decide the issue of women's membership.

Like Jim Davidson and Doug Howland, Curly had a passion for the extension of Rotary. When he completed his year as District governor (1973–74), he said that fourteen clubs would probably be chartered in the District in the coming year, based on the work during his presidential term. When he and his family were in Fiji, he spoke to a local Rotary Club there about the many great things Rotary was accomplishing worldwide. Years later, he would be approached by a man from Fiji, who told him of the effect his talk had on him. At the time of Curly's speech, the club was on the verge of calling it quits. After Curly's talk, they decided they should try again. They did and have been going strong ever since. Such were the powers of the man The Rotary Club of Calgary called "Mr. Rotary."

In Fellowship
AND Friendship

5

A boy is watching television and a voice comes from behind: "What are you watching?"

BOY: *"A new show about a super hero."*

PARENT: *"What does the super hero do?"*

BOY: *"He saves the world by going for lunch with his friends every Tuesday."*

PARENT: *"What's the show called?"*

BOY: *"Conan the Rotarian."*

IT WOULD BE CORRECT TO SAY that Rotary was born of a desire for friendship. When Paul Harris was practicing law in Chicago as a young man and felt he needed more fellowship in his life, he started the Rotary Club.

Rotary did not last long as a vehicle for fellowship alone. Service was soon added, and not just a casual form, but "Service Above Self." The two pillars of Rotary, fellowship and service, have been side by side ever since — or more than that: they have been inseparable. Few things bond people as tightly as working hard together on a common project.

A form of fundraiser for which The Rotary Club of Calgary is justly famous is the western barbecue, a labour-intensive activity if there ever was one. Most volunteers will tell you it is a lot of work and a lot of fun.

Once you've buttered a few hundred buns side by side with another person, the two of you are apt to know one another fairly well. That the wives of Rotarians have always assisted with the barbecues means that couples got to know one another too. Friendships between families blossomed.

Many Rotary group activities illustrate the same point. The Rotary show delivered at the annual President's Ball is another Rotary tradition that has drawn hundreds of people into friendship.

There has always been a subset of activities at Rotary that are purely for fellowship. Under this heading you find all the sports, games, picnics, dances, seasonal parties, and balls that comprise a Rotary year.

● ● ●

(LEFT) DON CAMPBELL sampling harvest corn at a Rotary Club Fall Fair. (RIGHT) CUTTING CHRISTMAS TREES at the Richard Copithorne Ranch, 1989.

THE HEART OF ROTARY FELLOWSHIP is the weekly luncheon. At the Tuesday lunch, members meet, eat, and sing. They catch up on club news, have a few laughs, and hear from an interesting speaker — all within an hour and fifteen minutes.

For much of the club's history, attendance at luncheons was a serious matter. If a member's attendance fell below a certain threshold, there was trouble. Even being on the road was not sufficient excuse for not attending a weekly meeting. In another city or town, you were to find the local Rotary Club and attend its lunch in lieu of your own.

The most stunning record for attendance belongs to Curly Galbraith who managed a perfect attendance record for fifty-two years! Curly's wife Doris says there was no rounding off involved either. Whereas others might have thought it difficult to attend Rotary while travelling, Curly told Doris, "It's not hard. You just have to plan ahead." Another member with an admirable attendance record is Jim Jenkins: 100-percent attendance from April 1977 to May 2009.

The modern club's view of attendance is not as strict as it used to be. For example, committee work is now regarded as a replacement for attendance. To quote 2013–14 president, Eva Friesen, "Engagement, not attendance, is the focus." The quality of a member's engagement is more important than how often he or she comes to lunch.

A major tradition of The Rotary Club of Calgary is that its luncheons take place at the Fairmont Palliser Hotel. Calgary's original Rotary Club and the Palliser have grown up together. The Rotary Club of Calgary has been trooping down to the Palliser for most Tuesdays of its one-hundred-year history.

THE CLUB'S TUESDAY LUNCHEON at the Fairmont Palliser Hotel lies at the heart of club fellowship: where friendships are made and maintained, where good humour and club business are mixed.

The whole idea of a Rotary Club lunch is that it should not vary much in structure. Members gather at lunchtime, collect their food from the buffet, and take a seat. At noon, the head-table guests enter. The club piano player plays, and the members clap them in. On Robbie Burns Day, there might be a piper.

If the house is unruly, the president brings members to attention with a gavel whack on the club's gong. The club's oldest artifact is a gong that was fashioned from the bell of the city's first fire wagon. It still attends meetings but has been deemed too venerable for gavel whacking. Another gong is used for calls to order.

"O Canada" is sung heartily. The singing of the anthem and other songs at lunch had better be good or the lack will be mentioned.

Head table guests are introduced, including the day's speaker. Guests from other clubs are also recognized. It is common for members from other clubs, even international ones, to drop by. As well, members bring a guest now and again: exchange students, persons who have won a club-sponsored award, representatives accepting a club donation, and persons who have been given permission to announce a good cause.

Family members are sometimes invited. In the days of men-only Rotary, club wives attended the Valentine's Day lunch, the Christmas lunch, and were also invited whenever there was a speaker of particular interest.

Among special-occasion lunches, a favourite has always been the Calgary Stampede luncheon, partly because it features performers from the Grandstand Show.

Birthdays are recognized at lunch, as are illnesses, this being the job of the secretary to the president. Deaths are announced and short eulogies given.

The Programs Committee selects the speakers and works months in advance to ensure they are topical, capable, and available in Calgary on that day. Speakers are selected for any number of reasons, but some relate to a calendar event or anniversary. On the closest Tuesday to Remembrance Day, the speaker is often a veteran or serving member of the armed forces. Sometimes a club clergyman will address world peace. If Stampede time is coming up, the top brass at the Exhibition and Stampede might drop by. Effort is made to not ignore the good speaking talent of the club's own members.

Visiting politicians have been a staple of the Rotary lunch. Calgary's mayors traditionally attend a club lunch in January to give a "state of the union" address. The press often attends. Ralph Klein visited regularly in his years as mayor and continued to do so after joining the provincial cabinet. As Alberta's premier, he visited still. Calgary native son Peter Lougheed also visited downtown Rotary lunches throughout his amazing career.

A list of the speakers at club luncheons reads like a historical timeline. On July 5, 1922, Governor General Lord Byng visited the club. In 1924, Wallace Laycock of Imperial Oil spoke about the petroleum potential of Alberta. In 1928, famous dinosaur-hunter Professor Charles M. Sternberg addressed the club about his summer's work in the badlands. Arctic Explorer Vilhjamur Stefansson spoke in 1929. In 1930, bestselling author Ralph Connor entertained.

A memorable luncheon took place at the Calgary Brewing Co. on November 5, 1935. Calgary Brewing offered the members lunch and beverages, and the club decided to charge members the usual seventy-five cents anyway, proceeds to community services. R. A. "Streetcar" Brown Sr., who ran the Calgary streetcar system (and a year later discovered oil under the gas cap at Turner Valley), offered the club a special car to take them to and from the brewery.

In 1942, Mrs. Ho Lem of Calgary spoke about the life of Mrs. Chiang Kai-shek. In 1943, a well-known Calgary native son, pilot Lt. W. H. Pedland, described flying operations over Europe. On June 6, 1944, at 1 pm, the club listened to the King's speech. In 1945, Pilot Officer Bob Dingman, son of Rotarian Charlie Dingman, described his two years as a prisoner of war.

In 1948, the Calgary Stampeders had the first undefeated CFL season and rolled to victory in the Grey Cup game against Ottawa. The Grey Cup was in Toronto, and a special trainload of Calgarians turned Toronto upside down for a week. Alderman Don Mackay rode a horse into the lobby of the Royal York Hotel. At the Rotary luncheon on December 7, 1948, Stampeders coach Les Lear introduced his team, and Don Mackay gave "an extremely interesting account of the train trip to Toronto and back."

The following year, a train-full of Torontonians returned the favour, coming west for the Stampede. Their float in Calgary's Stampede Parade was called "Toronto the Good." Calgary's Rotarians were asked to open their homes to the travellers, as the train on which they were staying had no bathing facilities.

In 1950, a speaker came to lunch to tell members about the phenomenon of television. At a special Coronation ceremony in 1953, Bishop George Calvert gave a toast to the new monarch, Queen Elizabeth II. In 1957, Calgary's director of Civil Defence spoke about a plan to evacuate Calgary in the event of an H-Bomb attack.

In 1967, Hon. Lester B. Pearson addressed the club as part of Canada's centennial year. In 1970, Peter Lougheed spoke about the Alberta Progressive Conservative Party of which he was leader. In 1972, Peter Lougheed's first speech to a service club as Alberta's premier was to The Rotary Club of Calgary.

* * *

ANOTHER TRADITION OF THE ROTARY LUNCH — which waxes and wanes — is humorous stunts. The first recorded humorous stunt at a Rotary Club of Calgary luncheon was a sawdust pie on April Fool's Day, 1916. The story goes that many a hungry Rotarian took a good mouthful and then had to figure out a way to get rid of it "in a graceful manner."

In 1936, Alex Ross, an inveterate practical joker, took over the Fellowship Committee. Ross made it obligatory for every new member of the club to be a member of his committee, and they met every second Monday to plan stunts for Tuesday lunch. Ross came up with something called the "Fine Wheel," a wheel of fortune for the punishing of club infractions. Members had, among other things, been failing to wear their name buttons to lunch. For the men with empty lapels, Ross spun his wheel to determine the amount of their fine.

Alex Ross was elected president the following year. He continued stunting. One of the traditions of the day was to have a lunchtime collection of quarters for club babies. One Tuesday, Ross announced there was a new baby in the home of Mr. and Mrs. Jones. Fellows dug in their pockets and dropped quarters in the passing hat. When they were done, Ross said, "Thanks, fellas.

There is no Jones family in the club, but the money will help fill up the community service fund." Another of his jokes was to cut off the speaker's tie while pronouncing his thanks.

It was inevitable that the jokers Ross had trained would make him the butt of a stunt some day. One of Ross's hallmarks was the fury with which he struck the gong to silence the crowd at luncheons. One week, he did so with customary aggression and the gong flew to pieces. (Luckily, the gong was a replica made of brittle material by his former protégés.)

Several club presidents have gone on to become District governors and directors and vice-presidents of Rotary International. One of those was Curly Galbraith. Curly had a habit of dropping by club luncheons to tell the club of new developments at RI. On one of those occasions, the instant Curly started to speak everyone picked up his newspaper and began to read.

Future federal minister and agriculturalist Harry Hays joined the club in 1950 and was a force in the club for the next two decades. Although he contributed many things and became president, his presence always meant good fun at lunches. In his presidential summary in 1950–51, Glen Peacock wrote:

> With prices continuing to rise, it was felt that Harry Hays could well have donated to each of the Board members large roasts each month. This failed to materialize and at Christmas a motion was passed asking him to supply each of the Board members with a turkey. That in turn failed to materialize.

• • •

A ROTARY STUNT: the lady in the babushka (Don Cushing) gives District Governor Galbraith the gift of a "baby."

CLUB SINGING

Back in 1914, when told that Rotary's luncheon tradition required a singsong, the founders of Rotary in Calgary gave it a go — but did not like it. Singing was not attempted again until 1916. In January 1926, the club published a song written by Maynard Joiner and Harry Hutchcroft. The idea was to print a hundred sheets of the song and sell them at the next District Conference. The name of the song was "Calgary."

IN 1951–52, outgoing president Charles Kennedy made reference to the club's program of visiting the sick with flowers provided gratis by J. W. Hughes of Kelowna for this purpose. "The only complaint registered in this respect," said Kennedy, "was from Holstein Hays who kept yelling for more flowers. After we discovered he was making them into corsages and boutonnieres and peddling them up and down the hall, we cut him off."

The early fifties seemed to have been a high-water mark for stunts. At a 1949–50 lunch, President Bill Snaddon had to act quickly to thwart an attack on a luncheon by "alleged Communists." Other times, a group of Hutterites, complete with geese would visit.

When Harry Hays was president, he and Grace Presbyterian Pastor Frank Morley got in the habit of exchanging barbs every Tuesday, the sharper the better. At the final lunch of Harry's year, Pastor Morley approached the head table and made an elaborate apology for his behaviour during the year. He handed Harry a gift-wrapped peace offering. Harry unwrapped the box, tipped up the lid, and abruptly left the room. The box contained a baby skunk, which was later returned to its parents at the Calgary Zoo.

One luncheon stunt happened not at the Palliser but at a Vancouver hotel. Holland Cameron, a past president of The Rotary Club of Calgary, had moved to Vancouver and hooked up with the downtown Rotary club there. Holland had soon convinced them to put on a Rotary show of the type that was traditional in Calgary. On the sly, Curly and Doris Galbraith, Swanny Swanson, and several other Calgary Rotarians flew to Vancouver where they suddenly appeared during the cocktail hour prior to the Vancouver Rotary show. Led by Rev. Swanson, they carried placards accusing Vancouver of stealing their writing and their acts. Holland Cameron had not been tipped off, and the stunt went well.

PETER KARSTON, seen here kissing a donkey at a club luncheon, was the director of the Calgary Zoo from 1974 to 1994 — as well as being a member of The Rotary Club of Calgary.

REV. SWANNY SWANSON

CHARLIE KENNEDY (left) and Rev. Swanny Swanson at Swanny's birthday lunch.

When Swanny Swanson returned to Calgary as Archdeacon of St. Stephen's Anglican Church, the colourful clergyman was asked to join The Rotary Club of Calgary. He was one of the club's most beloved members. In 1978, there was a lunch in Swanny's honour. The club band played "When that Saint Comes Marching In," and Rabbi Louis Ginsberg read a few of the Yukon days excerpts from Swanny's book of memoirs, *The Days of My Sojourning,* including the story about skinny-dipping on Dominion Day. On February 13, 1979, the club had a cake at lunch to celebrate Swanny's ninetieth birthday.

Another joker in the club was Dick Yetzer. He was very quick with a line, so it was just and natural that he should be made the butt of a practical joke some day. In 1985, Stan Sailer's year as president, the President's Ball and Show was in November. The Yetzers had decided they would stay overnight at the Palliser after the show. When they arrived to check in, club member Michael Broadhurst, who was manager of the Palliser, told them the room they had booked wasn't ready, but he had a "special" room arranged for them. A porter led them to the train station platform where a tent had been erected.

● ● ●

OVER ITS ONE HUNDRED YEARS, The Rotary Club of Calgary's fellowship events have come in all shapes and sizes. Club records suggest the first fellowship event was a family picnic at Bowness Park in 1916. John Bullough and the Grand Theatre Orchestra provided music for a club dinner dance in 1921 — with $22 going toward a "gross of Rotary hats." John Bullough became a club member before the year was out.

GLEN PEACOCK was president of The Rotary Club of Calgary in 1950–51. He went on to be a District governor and third vice-president of Rotary International.

The fact that The Rotary Club of Calgary's lunches — in fact, all Rotary functions — were "dry" for many decades led to a public impression that Rotary was an organization of temperance advocates. One suspects this was somewhat off the mark. All the same, Rotary functions stayed dry until 1956–57. Ironically, this was the year that Bert Dyson, who was in fact a teetotaler, was president. The word "cocktail" appears in club documents for the first time in 1958: in outgoing president John Stevenson's final report.

The club often staged dinner dances on Valentine's Day. In the depths of the depression, a ladies' night of cards and dancing was booked at the Palliser Hotel in May. Prior to the event, a club committee met with the hotel's manager to see if the cost could be reduced. Family events suffered during the depression. In 1933, a ladies' night dance was cancelled in favour of a picnic, and, when there was little interest in the picnic, that was cancelled too.

The Leduc oil discovery reversed Alberta's fortunes in 1947, and The Rotary Club of Calgary responded with an explosion of fellowship events. At the end of 1950-51, when summarizing his presidential year, Glen Peacock gave a list of activities that improved fellowship:

Old Folks Picnic at the Legion Hall; Rotary picnic at George Edworthy's Shaganappi Ranch; Inter-club golf tournament with High River and Banff; chest x-ray survey registration; bowling; table tennis; wind-up evening for table tennis; social evening and club anniversary celebration on March 26 at Penley Academy; Christmas Party with entertainment by the players of Workshop 14; church service at Maurice Brown's church (reception afterwards at Glencoe Club); Charles McKinnon's generous barbecue; Chuck Railton in charge of stunts; prize for winning stunt presented today; square dancing.

Charlie McKinnon's "generous barbecue," mentioned above, may have been the first Rotary Club of Calgary barbecue. McKinnon came from a legendary ranch: the L. K. Farm and Ranch Co. at Dalemead. In 1951–52, Harry and Muriel Hays produced the next club barbecue at Hays Farm on the southern outskirts of the city. Charles and Opal McKinnon were thanked for the donation of a whole steer to the event.

Hays Farm had a large herd of dairy cattle, which caused some Rotary wag to give Harry the nickname "Holstein" Hays. For many years thereafter, the barbecue at Hays Farm was an annual affair. In 1954–55, there were two Hays barbecues, one for the club and one for the District Conference.

In the 1970s, Curly and Doris Galbraith took up the mantle of the club barbecue staging one every summer for many years at their country home at Springbank. In the 1980s, friends of Rotary Ted and Lola Rozsa hosted the club barbecue and the fall fair at their ranch.

• • •

ANNIVERSARIES

Significant club anniversaries have always been occasions for fellowship and celebration. In 1922, New Year's and the eighth anniversary of the club were celebrated together in such style that an article was sent to *The Rotarian*:

> *Jeff Lydiatt's eight-year-old daughter, Grace, acted the part of Miss Rotary and ushered in the New Year. In startling contrast to the fresh sweetness of little Miss Lydiatt's attire, stood out the somber robes and death-dealing scythe of the living personification of the Grim Reaper — otherwise known as Harry Hutchcroft — who sang in doleful tones the grave-yard dirge of the death of the old year.*

The club's twenty-first anniversary fell in the middle of the depression, but a dinner and dance at the Palliser was held anyway. The hotel offered an orchestra for free. When the club turned twenty-five in 1939, they again celebrated at the Palliser. Three hundred Rotarians and their partners attended, taking in a March of Time pageant followed by bridge and dancing. The thirty-fifth anniversary, 1949, might have been the most fanciful. Father Time cut open a huge papier-mâché cake and out popped a 1914 giant baby in diapers — followed by a 1949 cowboy, with guns a-blazing.

For the fiftieth anniversary, in 1964, the organizing committee went with golden everything. A golden chair at lunch in which former presidents sat — one at a time. Ten "golden girls," daughters of club members, attended anniversary events, and of course it was the occasion of the fifty $500 scholarships to students at UAC. The seventy-fifth anniversary was celebrated with a booklet of club history. Stan Sailer was Anniversary Committee chair and Bill Gillott was vice-chair. The birthday party, as it was billed, took place on April 22, 1989, and the honoured guest was Rotary International President Royce Abbey, all the way from Australia.

As for the centennial anniversary of The Rotary Club of Calgary, in 2013–14, the main project is the book in your hands: a permanent record of the first one hundred years of the club's journey. On May 3, 2014, a gala was held at the Hyatt Hotel in Calgary to mark the centennial.

THE FIRST MENTION OF sport and games shows up in 1921–22: "Contests with other clubs have been inaugurated in bridge, golf, etc." Golf has always been the gold standard for Rotary sports. The golf trophies bore the names of early and founding members. In 1936, Walter Ripley won the D. E. Black Cup while Jack Jenkinson took away the Ardern Cup.

The first mention of club bowling appears in 1931, when an invitation to a Kansas City Rotary bowling tournament was turned down because the Calgary club "does not play 10-pin." Rotary's bowling league was one of the few club initiatives capable of turning a profit in the depression.

Bridge has been almost as popular and enduring in club history as golf. In the 1930s, bridge parties were held at different Rotary homes, with a charge of fifty cents a player, remitted to the club for community service.

By 1939, ping-pong had emerged as a Rotary sport, with its own leagues. The popularity of the sports leagues can be gauged from the fact that, in 1946, new Rotary members could not get into the bowling league because the teams were full.

In many of these sports, the Rotary Anns (Rotary wives) had parallel leagues. This led, in 1946–47, to a bowling tournament pitting male Rotarians against the Anns. A summary of the Rotary Anns year included this note: "The ladies enjoyed a happy season of bowling, held several luncheons, completed considerable work in their Red Cross group, and completely swamped the men in the bowling wind-up." In 1954–55, the men finally won this bowling tournament, and, hence, were willing to make it an annual event. In 1960–61, curling joined the sporting parade.

Windup parties for the various sports leagues were spirited affairs, celebrated to the hilt. In April 1938, a weekly letter mentioned the bowlers' banquet at the Renfrew Club, and asked this question: "Will the bowler who, by mistake of course, carried off a flowering plant, please return it to the Rotary Club next Tuesday?"

• • •

DISTRICT CONFERENCES were another good occasion for fellowship. In Alex Ross's year as president, 1937–38, he was annoyed that, with just a couple of weeks to go, sixty of his members had not registered for the District Conference in Banff. He told the lunch crowd:

> It is too many. In order to make this conference a success, we must have 100 percent registration. Very complete plans have been made for the entertainment of the ladies, including golf, drives, bridge, and dances, and there will not be an idle moment if they wish to avail themselves of the entertainment provided. We want as many of our ladies present as possible.

So too is the annual Rotary International Conference an occasion for global fellowship. Though the majority of RI Conferences have occurred in the United States, the number of conferences in other countries rose as Rotary became more international. The Rotary Club of Calgary pays for its president and secretary to travel to the conference every year, but a surprising number of members show up at RI Conferences on their own nickel.

• • •

THE WORLD CONFERENCE OF ROTARY INTERNATIONAL, CALGARY, 1996

A major milestone in club history came in 1996 when The Rotary Club of Calgary hosted the Rotary International Conference. Because of Calgary's proximity to the United States, the Calgary RI conference was expected to be one of the biggest in Rotary history. Everything was on a large scale: two barbecues, one planned for up to six thousand and the second for up to twelve thousand; a lunch at the Olympic Oval; and plenary sessions in the Saddledome. Club members cheerfully recall two things: that it was the most convivial RI conference in their memory and that the weather was terrible. The conference was so good the weather scarcely seemed to matter.

THIS ALL-STAR TEAM of Rotary Club of Calgary luncheon goers symbolizes the Rotary/Flames Reach! partnership that kicked off in 2005.

THE APPEAL OF ANY ORGANIZATION has to reside, finally, in the self. If a person feels improved through belonging, he or she will continue, and, if the person feels the same or less, he or she will not continue. Across time and across a large group of people, this effect, positive or negative, will determine the lifespan of the organization: whether it has legs or stops. In 2014, with the Rotary movement at age 109 and The Rotary Club of Calgary at 100, the evidence that Rotary membership is a positive experience is overwhelming.

One of the keys to that success was Paul Harris's initial understanding that people need fellowship first and other fulfillments afterwards. The emphasis on fellowship has created countless friendships, legendary friendships, and friendships not just between members but between and among their families too. That is, membership in The Rotary Club of Calgary has always offered an experience that is whole: play and work, friendship and fulfillment, fun and achievement — all in a single package.

No wonder the club has survived and thrived, and is headed into its second century.

FLOWERS FOR THE LIVING

Between 1951 and 1969, J. W. Hughes of Kelowna sent thousands of tulips, peonies, and gladioli to The Rotary Club of Calgary for distribution to shut-ins. In 1968, at a Rotary luncheon, Mr. Hughes was given a plaque to honour this amazing contribution.

The September 30, 1959, *Free Press Weekly* profiled Mr. Hughes in an article called "The Business of Bees." He was originally from Iowa but had moved to Olds, Alberta, in 1908 and then to Kelowna in 1917, where he began commercial cultivation of grapes in 1926. He started growing flowers in 1933 and began sending blooms through Rotary Clubs to shut-ins in prairie cities in 1948.

The Tides of History

6

THE FIRST FOUR DECADES of The Rotary Club of Calgary included two world wars and the century's worst and longest economic depression. The 1920s was the only decade of the club's youth that was relatively free of catastrophe.

This debut was a thorough grounding in a fact of Rotary life: that no Rotary Club exists outside history. Nor should it. A service club divorced from the tides of history and economy would be of little use. It would not live up to the full expression of service that is the basis and meaning of Rotary.

THE CHOICE TO CREATE A ROTARY CLUB in Calgary was rooted in feelings of prosperity and potential. Calgary had been growing by leaps and bounds when local businessmen met in Cronn's Rathskeller in 1914 to plan a Rotary Club. While it was true that the real estate boom faltered in 1913, any booster worth his salt would have called it a temporary hiccup while remaining certain that Calgary's future was bright.

On August 4, 1914, Britain declared war on Germany, and Canada went to war in support of its mother country. The first members of the Canadian Expeditionary Force landed in Britain in October.

All over Canada, young men poured into enlistment offices. Albertans were no different. By the end of the Great War, over forty-five thousand Albertans had enlisted.

The number of Calgarians in the war was approximately forty-five hundred. Of these about one in ten would die.

Though Rotary's stance has always been to avoid taking positions in politics, it does not prohibit local clubs from doing what is natural for them. In time of war, Rotarians have a history of supporting their fighting troops. The support tends to go toward the health of soldiers and the well-being of their families, and into the buying of Victory Bonds and Loans. The first mention of the club's support for the Great War was money raised in 1916–17 for St. Dunstan's Hospital for blind soldiers and sailors.

In Donald B. Smith's *Calgary's Grand Story*, he describes the Lougheed Building as a hub of war-related activity. Senator James Lougheed, owner of

CALGARY'S GRAND THEATRE was a hub of war-related activity during World War I. Theatre owner, Sir James Lougheed, invited Canadian servicemen to come to the shows at his theatre for free.

the building, extended the offer that all soldiers at local military camps were welcome at his Grand Theatre for free. In 1916, Prime Minister Borden came to Calgary for a giant rally in support of the war, also at the Grand.

Sadly, the restaurant in the Lougheed Building basement, Cronn's, fell victim to anti-German emotion. Donald Smith writes that one group came to Cronn's determined to wreck it, because Mr. and Mrs. Cronn were of German extraction, while another group assembled to defend it. That night, Mr. and Mrs. Cronn left town.

Jeff Lydiatt, manager of the Grand Theatre, was the club's president in 1917–18. In addition to entertaining troops at the Grand, Mr. Lydiatt was busy raising money for Europe through the YMCA. He also chaired the Salvation Army's Red Shield campaign. Club history says that, in 1917–18, Calgary's Rotary Club "led in the Victory Bond campaign."

On December 6, 1917, a collision with a munitions ship in Halifax Harbour caused an explosion that killed two thousand people, injured another nine thousand, and destroyed a large section of the city. Rotary led the drive in Calgary to collect funds for relief of Halifax.

In the summer of 1918, The Rotary Club of Calgary put on a huge picnic for the families of soldiers overseas. Six hundred automobiles transported people to St. George's Island. The crowd grew to fourteen thousand. Twelve thousand ice cream cones were consumed and fifty barrels of cider. Two thousand feet of film were shot of soldiers' wives and children waving at the camera and tossing their caps in the air. The idea was to show the film, titled *Hello Dad*, to Calgary troops overseas. They could search for their wives and children in the crowd. What a morale booster it must have been.

That same fall, a fresh disaster, unrelated to war, struck Calgary: the Spanish Flu Epidemic. In present-day parlance, this outbreak would be called a pandemic: a serious life-threatening illness, highly communicable, and without any known prevention or cure. It was called the Spanish Flu, not because it originated in Spain or was more terrible there, but because Spain was one of the few countries in Europe that did not suppress information about the epidemic.

Alberta's first case of Spanish Flu occurred in Calgary in October 1918. Schools, churches, and theatres were closed for the next month. The Rotary Club provided forty cars, working day and night, to transport Calgary nurses to and from work. In the end, fifty thousand Canadians died of the Spanish Flu: 341 in Calgary. The period of quarantine overlapped the end of World War I (November 11, 1918). The restriction on public gatherings was briefly suspended for a victory parade.

Calgary's Rotary Club planned a gigantic Christmas party for the wives and children of overseas soldiers the following month. Jim Davidson chaired the Entertainment Committee that hosted eighteen hundred children and twelve hundred mothers at the Calgary Exhibition Grounds. It was the only place with a building tall enough for the magnificent Christmas tree Rotary members had harvested. The retelling of the story has enlarged the tree to a point where many feel its stated height is impossible. A sixty-foot spruce tree! The truth is in there somewhere.

● ● ●

The failure of a company or the loss of one's job could force a resignation. But before accepting such resignations, the club president met with the member to see if something could be worked out. Sometimes, the club held a member's classification open in hopes that his business problem would resolve itself.

In January 1933, the club took action to protect its membership numbers by lowering annual dues from $30 to $25. The president of the day claimed that several "Scotsmen" joined who had been waiting for such an occasion. Another depression story is that a special club committee went to see the manager of the Palliser to ask if the cost of lunch could be reduced. The manager said it was not possible, but, in recognition of the times, agreed to make the club's office in the Palliser rent-free.

When the depression took hold, it hit the club from several directions. Resignations subtracted from dues and from the vigour of the club. The straitened economy meant it was ever harder to fundraise.

As the financial situation worsened, several strong advocates for social justice and relief for the poor approached the club. Past president Dr. George Kerby came asking for funds for the Canadian National Institute for the Blind — and was turned down. Nellie McClung came in person to appeal on behalf of the Unemployed Young Men and Girls Association. President Ernie Richardson gave her the standard answer: the club's major activity policy — playgrounds — had taken all the funds. In 1932, club stalwart Alex Hornibrook moved that all donation requests be refused until such time as there was new money. When someone suggested the Calgary club do something about the root causes of the depression, a spokesman answered: "Rotary does not care to meddle with economic questions."

Even if the Rotary Club board was clear about its approach to the depression, having to refuse those so obviously in need must have been unpleasant. Outside the club, members were asked why the Rotary Club wasn't doing more. In late November 1931, Alberta's former premier Hon. Herbert Greenfield asked to speak to the club on behalf of National Emergency Relief Week (December 10–17). After his appeal, club members threw themselves behind the National Emergency Relief drive, raising $6,250 in the first month.

If the club could not fund the many requests coming out of hard times, it did pass the appeals on to its members: for used clothing for parents who, though not on relief, could not provide their children's needs; for donations of books to relief camps the government had set up for unemployed men; for used skates for unemployed men; for the Waitress' Relief Committee wanting support during its strike.

MARY JANE POGUE volunteers at the Seniors' Christmas Party — a Rotary Club of Calgary tradition through good times and hard times.

Beyond Boys' Work and playgrounds, the club did maintain commitments to the poor. That is, whatever they were doing prior to the depression, they continued to do during the depression. The club kept up its role in the Old Folks' Picnic and its work with the Red Cross on preparation and delivery of Christmas hampers. It provided the supplies that Dr. McIntyre used in his free dental work at Wood's Homes.

• • •

THOUGH THE ROTARY CLUB DID ITS BEST to refrain from expressing political opinions, it is fair to say that most Rotary businessmen leaned in a conservative direction. Their opinions tended to be those of R. B. Bennett, who became Canada's Conservative prime minister in 1930. Before that, he had been a Calgary lawyer and a frequent and popular speaker at Rotary lunches.

If to be a conservative means protecting existing institutions, then Alberta Social Credit — the political movement that swept to provincial power in 1935 — was conservatism's opposite. Led by Calgary high school principal William Aberhart, Social Credit was a political reform movement from Britain. Aberhart's version of the doctrine included an Alberta currency and an Alberta bank that would free the province of the hated eastern and international banks he blamed for the hard times. For Aberhart, the depression was "poverty in the midst of plenty," and he offered Albertans $25 per month to reset the balance. Many of Premier Aberhart's reforms, including the $25 a month dividend, did not materialize. Canada's Supreme Court deemed other Alberta reforms illegal. Still, Social Credit remained Alberta's ruling party for the next thirty-six years.

Social Credit's radical financial plans seemed likely to play havoc with the lives of businessmen. The way Calgary's Rotary Club expressed disfavour was primarily through silence. Whereas national and provincial political leaders and representatives were usually welcome as speakers at Rotary luncheons, the leaders and representatives of Alberta Social Credit either were not invited or would not come. The only Social Credit premier at a Rotary Club of Calgary luncheon was Premier Ernest C. Manning, who succeeded William Aberhart in 1943. By the time Premier Manning spoke to Rotary (1953–54), he had been at the helm for many years and was a proven advocate of Alberta industry.

While it is true that William Aberhart never spoke to Calgary's Rotary Club as premier, a little-known fact is that he did speak at a club lunch while he was principal of Crescent Heights High School. He joined two other Calgary educators to discuss why boys were prone to leave school.

• • •

IN OCTOBER 1935, The Rotary Club of Calgary made a decision that helped the local unemployed. The YMCA asked the club for $250 per month for six months to support a program called Leisure Time League, and, surprisingly, the club agreed. It is surprising because the money was a lot for the time, and because the club was reluctant to invest in anything that required a long commitment. The recommendation came through the club's own Boys' Work Committee. Leisure Time League (a definite euphemism) did help teenagers, but it also assisted unemployed men of all ages.

In October 1936, the club received a report on the first year of the Leisure Time League. The league had provided "recreational, educational, and inspirational facilities for up to five hundred men." The men were permitted to use YMCA facilities from 9:30 to 4:30 on weekdays. They had classes in twenty-four group activities. One standard course was in first aid, and that added qualification had allowed fifty men to find employment in mines and lumber camps. Seventy received training in radio theory, and that too led to jobs. Rotary Club members also provided some with part-time work.

Frank Freeze, a Rotarian, came to a board meeting as a representative of the Board of Trade and asked the club to get involved in another depression program. To alleviate poverty in the cities, families had been moved to farms: the Back to the Land Movement. Frank Freeze's idea was to gather up clothes and other donations and take them to the people who had been able to stay on the farms. Again Rotary agreed to help.

The club's president in 1936–37 was J. S. "Jack" McMurchy. He was born in Glasgow, and the *COG* newsletter referred to him as "our first 100% Scotchman to hold the position of president." McMurchy was also the first president to loudly challenge the club to define itself in terms of important world issues.

In the November 3, 1937, issue of *COG*, McMurchy wrote a byline piece called "Is Rotary a Nebulous Thing?"

Rotary has been somewhat of a cloudy, hazy quantity suspended in the air without a very definite tie in its relationship to things on earth and to the practical questions of the moment . . . I am very definitely of the opinion that we, as an international brotherhood, should be voicing our beliefs and convictions in all matters where there is undoubtedly a right and a wrong . . . In the field of war, we have the spectre of wholesale murder of non-combatants yet Rotary is apparently afraid to voice itself against such dastardly conduct on the part of one of its member nations. Why? In recent years we have stood by and witnessed equally disturbing matters throughout the realm of nations having membership in Rotary and no voice from Rotary has been raised in protest . . . Rotary needs to take up and live a fuller and more definite life.

Jack McMurchy was talking about the Spanish Civil War and the rise of European fascism. Most Canadians fighting in Spain were volunteers in the International Brigades. Many of them had been unemployed during the depression. Some Rotarians felt as Jack McMurchy did: that the Canadians fighting the fascists in Spain (and the German fascists who supported the Spanish ones) were doing what the whole nation should be doing; which, in fact, the whole nation would be doing in 1939.

But, still, McMurchy's article was shockingly outside the Rotary playbook on political involvement, and some members said as much. In April 1938, a suggestion that a speaker address the club lunch on the "Spanish question"

was denied. Jack McMurchy remained a popular and effective president and finished his term without challenge.

McMurchy's question, though controversial, was a good one. Should Rotary Clubs play a role in the politics of nations and the world, rather than just supporting their country once it was at war? Should Rotary have been using its international influence, in countries like Spain and Germany, to confront the rise of fascism at an earlier stage?

These questions would have to wait, because the Spanish Civil War was indeed the precursor of a much larger war. Hitler began his campaign of expansion, and, when the German army invaded Poland on September 1, 1939, it touched off another twentieth-century world war.

As tensions rose and the world divided into enemy camps, Rotary's world faced its own trials. In Italy, fascist leader Benito Mussolini had disbanded the Rotary Clubs in his country in 1938. Hitler would do the same in Germany.

Maurice Brown was club president in 1939. That summer, he had to decide what to do about a Passion Play tour that several Rotary Clubs, including Calgary's, were supporting. In August, he circulated a note asking other District clubs what should be done if war broke out and the German cast could not enter Canada.

On August 29, 1939, President Brown spoke to the club lunch about the grave international crisis. The members sang three verses of "O Canada," stood for a moment of silence, then listened to Rev. Swanny Swanson say a prayer for peace.

When war was declared in September, the club met to decide what actions it should take. Rotary and Kiwanis cooperated on the purchase of twenty-five radios for army huts at Mewata Park. A members' collection raised money for a Heintzman piano, also for Mewata, where the

Calgary Highlanders awaited deployment to Europe. At Christmas, the club ordered inscribed penknives for all sons of Calgary Rotarians who had enlisted to fight. Club members were jumping into the war in many capacities. Pete Shields enlisted as commander of the RCASC (Royal Canadian Army Service Corps), First Division. Wilf Baker took command of the 4th divisional petrol company for the RCASC. Joe Ross became district recruiting officer. When Jim Corley left for England, his Rotary Club fellow members turned out at the CPR station to cheer him on his way. Later in the war, oilman Bob Brown, son of R.A. Brown, asked for leave from the club to join the Royal Canadian Naval Volunteer Reserve.

Perhaps the most famous single incident in the club's support of the war came at Tuesday lunch when funds were requested for an ambulance for our troops in Europe. In *five minutes*, club members produced $2,175. This more than paid for the ambulance, and months later the balance was used to purchase another ambulance for the relief effort in Greece.

Another great contribution to the war was spearheaded not by Calgary's Rotary Club members but by their wives. In October 1939, several wives joined a Red Cross plan to sew for the war effort. They came to Rotary for a contribution toward equipment. As the need arose, more electric sewing machines were purchased on Rotary's tab. When the women needed new rooms to work in, Rotary found the space. In mid-1941, Rotary wife Mrs. Fred Weir, president of the Ladies Red Cross Auxilliary, reported that their group had sewn 2,580 articles including 200 seamen's coats and 246 knitted articles.

● ● ●

A DIAMOND-STUDDED OPPORTUNITY to raise money for the war came when Mrs. Southcott of Maple Bay, Vancouver Island, donated a diamond bracelet and a diamond pendant for a Rotary Club of Calgary raffle. In a campaign headed by Oscar Rinman, club members sold tickets to other clubs, at military canteens, at a bull sale — basically, everywhere. The draw took place in early May and the winners attended a Rotary luncheon to collect their jewellery. The funds were divided between Canadian War Services and the Lord Mayor of London Fund. R. B. Bennett presented the cheque to the Lord Mayor of London in that city.

Around this time, the club received a letter from the Canadian Army Overseas, 18th Field Ambulance Corps to say that the "Rotary Ambulance" was with their company and in constant use.

The British Commonwealth Air Training Plan had a training school at Calgary's municipal airport, to which Rotary contributed a piano. Members also picked up the flyboys on Sundays to run them out to the mountains for sightseeing.

No one could accuse Calgary's Rotary Club of not committing fully enough to the war, as it continued to pour most of its funds and energy into war support. Inevitably, this included writing letters of sympathy to parents of soldiers killed overseas. Club members also attended the unveiling of a cairn dedicated to two American trainee airmen killed in a crash near Cochrane. As time went by, support would include sending parcels to Canadian prisoners of war. When each new round of Victory Loans went on sale, club members bought them avidly.

Finally, in May 1945, the European war ended with Germany's surrender to the Allies. Three months later, the Pacific War with Japan would end after American atomic bombs fell on Hiroshima and Nagasaki.

To celebrate VE Day, the club published a booklet listing eighty-six sons of Calgary Rotarians in the services, four daughters, and eleven Rotary Club members. Three were prisoners of war and five were missing.

• • •

THE TWO WORLD WARS and the global depression on which The Rotary Club of Calgary teethed set the stage for the club's future work. Two world wars in half a century catastrophically proved that peace could not be left to chance. It required a world network of communication and cooperation, something that Rotary could help to attain. Rotary International set out to rebuild the parts of its circuitry that had been destroyed by the conflict and, as always, tried to extend outward.

Naturally and inevitably, The Rotary Club of Calgary would go on responding to the twists and turns of economy and history as further decades passed, but there would be a whole new side to the organization devoted to solving international problems and forging international friendships. Thanks to globe-trotting Calgary Rotarians like James Wheeler Davidson and Doug Howland, few clubs in Rotary's world were better equipped for this future than The Rotary Club of Calgary.

The Heart
OF Fundraising

7

FUNDRAISING AND COMMUNITY WORK are where "service above self" is proven by any Rotary Club. The Rotary Club of Calgary's first fundraiser was a minstrel show. Forty-eight Rotarians dressed up, sang, and raised $1,607 in 1917. The shows went on for years, producing similar amounts for community service. In 1922, Sunshine Apple Day was added. Again, the Rotarians dressed up, as London costermongers with barrows and "mokes" (donkeys).

MEMBERS OF THE CLUB were always a little uncomfortable handing out charity. They favoured large projects like a playground that would bear the club's name for years. Many preferred to leave the small requests to government and charities.

But requests from individuals can be heartbreaking — especially if your policy is to refuse them. The result was that the club often buckled. For example, in 1922, the board sent out an appeal for used furniture for Mrs. Brenner who was burned out in south Calgary. During a coal shortage that winter, the club often checked the supply at the convalescent home in Mount Royal.

The issue of whether the club should meet various demands or focus on "one major activity" soon came to a head. C. O. Smith pushed for the latter, and his motion must have passed, because, in April 1924, the club had a Major Activity Committee weighing three proposals: a baby clinic, a YMCA project, and a school for tuberculosis prevention.

THIS HUPMOBILE was the prize raffle attraction at a Rotary Calgary "Potlatch" in 1924.

One of the most unusual club fundraisers took place in 1924. It was called a "potlatch" (the West Coast Native word for giveaway), which was a misnomer in that Rotary wasn't giving anything but intended to sell and auction goods.

Even the potlatch location was strange: a basement excavation on 9th Avenue and 1st Street S. Chief of Police Dave Ritchie collected tickets and Rev. Dr. Bingham raffled hams. Rotary historian John Boyd's note on the subject says that Rev. Bingham's presence cost club president Reuban Ward the donation of a carpet to the Baptist church.

The grand prize of the potlatch was a Hupmobile, valued at over $2,000. This automobile was made in Detroit between 1909 and 1940. Here's a sample of the advertising: "There's something about Hupp's faithfulness that gets to a man. A feeling that hasn't a name. But it's the same as the feeling a seaman gets for his ship, an engineer for his engine, or a woman for her home."

The potlatch yielded $14,822: a club record.

In the late twenties, another car was auctioned. When the successful bidder got home, he found a problem, something about improper drainage and freezing while in storage. The buyer of a horse came back with complaints too. Art McGuire solved that by selling the animal, but the car issue refused to die. The purchaser was finally given back his money.

It is noteworthy how often Calgary Rotary Club community service involved cars. The frequency of transport requests may have had to do with Rotarians being early adopters of the automobile. They drove nurses during the Spanish Flu panic, carried veterans home from the train station after the Armistice, drove soldiers from the Colonel Belcher Hospital to the

ROY THOMPSON'S SEEING-EYE DOG

In 1937, Calgary's Rotary Club committed funds so that member Roy Thompson could get a seeing-eye dog. When, many years later, Roy's dog, Wanda, died, the club voted unanimously to buy him another seeing-eye canine.

mountains, and picked up seniors for the *Calgary Herald* Sunshine Fund picnics.

Perhaps the best transportation story ever was when a Rotarian took an elderly woman out for a spin. "Where would you like to go?" he asked, and she replied, "I want to go on the north highway — at ninety miles per hour." Being a good Rotarian, he complied.

• • •

DURING THE DEPRESSION, the club's executive secretary wore her fingers to nubs typing two words: "No funds." The club kept up its commitments but did little new. A true sign of austerity was when a boy scout lost his leg and the club offered a "loan" of $25.

In the thirties, the club had one solid fundraising success: a show called the *Sunset Revue* in which members performed. Profits from the first show equipped two playgrounds. Proceeds from the second went to the Countess of Bessborough's Cancer Fund.

The club worked hard to set up a coherent system for deciding major donations, but the depression made it difficult. For example, the club chose a city swimming pool in memory of the late King. When the estimate came in high, and the city was not even sure it could afford to own a pool, the idea was dropped.

The 1936 Donation Committee suggested two causes: Red Cross Crippled Children's Hospital and the Shriners Hospital for Crippled Children. Both had to wait for the raising of funds. A touring exhibition, Sir Neville Wilkinson's Titania's Palace, saved the day. The miniature castle came about because Wilkinson's daughter felt sorry for wood faeries who had to live in caves. Titania's Palace had eighteen rooms, lavishly furnished and decorated with tiny artworks. By backing the exhibition, the club raised funds for both crippled children's hospitals.

• • •

THE RETURN TO WAR IN 1939 meant that most funds would go to support soldiers and their families. But a donation game-changer did occur in 1940. The Rotary Club had been trying since the twenties to get a Community Chest for Calgary: a funding body to accept money from service organizations and pay it out to charities.

For a long time, Community Chest simmered but would not boil. Maurice Brown, Fred Stapells, and Clarence Tait are the Calgary Rotarians credited with bringing the cause to fruition after a decade of meetings.

On the money-raising front, the next idea was a Hereford calf sale in conjunction with the Hereford Breeders Association. The Breeders wanted to give 50 percent of proceeds to Red Cross and 25 percent to the Merchant Marine. The rest could go to war services as chosen by Rotary. Rotary's committee for the sale was Jim Cross, Charles Yule, and Sher Willows.

The success of the calf sale made the club "bullish" on fundraising. In October 1943, Calgary Rotary bought a house to raffle. It was on the city's North Hill and cost $8,500. The purchase was no small feat given a wartime housing shortage. Tickets were one dollar. Alf Duffin was in charge.

By November 16, tickets were ready for distribution. The club was nervous and cranked up publicity. Advertising was extended to all of Alberta and Saskatchewan. A typical ad read: "It can be yours! Completely furnished. Seven spacious rooms including model kitchen with nook and games room. Double garage. Air conditioned and controlled heat."

As the draw date neared, tickets started selling in such numbers that the board worried about the venture's legality. In the end, a stunning $65,000 was netted back to the club. There were many potential takers for the windfall, but the club stuck to its original plan: a new building for

Rotary Boys' Town. Even though wartime supply authorities would not let them build, they held the money for that purpose.

In 1948, influenced by the success of the Shrine Circus, Rotary decided to try its hand at being a circus impresario. Leish McNeill, Merv Cozart, and Gordon McGachie were among the members who pulled it together. The report read: "Instead of just breaking even, as had been the anticipated result, our first venture in the realm of the saw-dust ring realized an estimated $3,901 profit."

The following year the club ran another circus, but its report was less buoyant. "We had a tremendous amount of outside competition, including Army Week. While we will have a small loss in operating this circus, our members did get better acquainted ... and had a lot of fun and fellowship that would otherwise not have been possible."

In 1949–50, the club proved that "third time lucky" is not an infallible axiom. They tried another circus and lost more money. Members dug in their pockets and reduced the deficit. President William Snaddon summed up as follows: "It would appear that circuses are not the answer to our prayers in connection with community service."

IN 1943, DURING A PROFOUND WAR-TIME HOUSING SHORTAGE, the club was able to buy and raffle the house depicted on this ticket. The raffle raised an unprecedented $65,000 for community service. The funds raised went toward the construction of a new building for Rotary Boys' Town.

Major fundraising has never been a simple business. In his report on 1950–51, outgoing president Glen Peacock explained why there was no major fundraiser that year:

> We were assured that the oil show . . . would prove an outstanding attraction. Eventually the oil companies, partly in view of the shortage of steel and the restrictive regulations resulting from war developments, felt there was no point in going ahead . . . We then attempted an auto show without success. We were prepared to sponsor The Navy Show . . . when that was postponed. We thought that various other attractions . . . would be under Rotary sponsorship, such as the Happy Gang, but this too failed to materialize.

Next, the club supported the Junior Football Merry-Go-Round. Football spectators being less fickle than circus-goers, this mutual promotion for Rotary and junior football succeeded. For several years, the event realized around $3,000 per annum. In 1955–56, the club returned to concert promotion, backing a successful Wilf Carter show.

Around this time, the club got the idea of making decorative licence plates. Twenty thousand were made, each inscribed: "I was at the Calgary Stampede." People could mount them below their real licence plates.

Teams of Rotary salesmen poured into the Stampede parking lot only to discover the people with the cars were not at their cars but in the grandstand watching the rodeo. There was also the fact that the words on the little plates were too small to read unless you were a foot away. The plates were reduced to a dollar, then to fifteen cents, then given away to anyone who would take one.

ROTARY WRESTLING NIGHT

In 1957, wrestling promoter Stu Hart spoke to The Rotary Club of Calgary about a wrestling night in aid of the Alberta Crippled Children's Hospital. All the club had to do was pick a Friday wrestling night at the Stampede Corral and give Hart the first $5,000 to pay the wrestlers. The children's hospital could have the rest.

To promote the event, the club entertained Stu Hart and fifteen of his "grapplers" at lunch. For the *Calgary Herald* cameraman, two behemoths known as the Miller Brothers gave wrestling night chairman Cliff Walker "a lift." As for the night itself, some had been worried that pro wrestling might not be suitable for Rotary families. Except for their seats being very close, and giants like the Miller Brothers spilling out of the ring into those seats, a good time was had by all.

The wrestling night drew 4,674 people, and made $24,733 for the Crippled Children's Hospital — including a donation from Stu Hart. In some dark corner is a film called *The Brightest Jewel in the Crown of Rotary*, shot that night. It was shown at the Rotary lunch on January 3, 1959.

IN 1951, when club families were having a brilliant time at a fellowship at Hays Farm on Calgary's southern outskirts, it is doubtful anyone thought it was the advent of Rotary's most reliable fundraiser — but that is the truth.

The family barbecue became an annual club event, and out of the fun came a powerful idea. Why not stage a barbecue in connection with the Calgary Stampede and call it a Rotary fundraiser? This happened for the first time in 1957 at Mewata Stadium and cleared a tidy sum.

For the second Stampede Barbecue, the club needed more equipment. It was on the verge of commissioning two giant ovens when Harry Hays said the club could use his oven, which could barbecue two thousand pounds of beef. The only problem was that Harry's oven was currently in Ontario. The club was in a pinch: order two ovens or gamble on Harry's. They gambled, and the oven made it in time. The need soon arose for the club to commission its own ovens.

BILL GANT taking a break during a Stampede Barbecue. Bill was club president, District governor, and, in 1993–94, a director of Rotary International.

In the first five years, the Stampede Barbecue at Mewata netted an average of $4,058. Already in 1958, the Barbecue Committee had branched out to cater a non-Stampede barbecue (for the Shriners). In 1962, they did another for Presto Gas. The club at this point had no official way of transporting the gear necessary for the smaller catered barbecues, and club members themselves packed the gear into pickup trucks.

By now, the volunteer group of Rotarians and their wives had barbecuing for hundreds down to a science. Each year they prepared an updated multi-paged mimeograph of instructions. The safety rules for food handling were stringent — although there is a story about a Rotary Ann mixing coleslaw bare-handed and realizing at the end of the day that all her red nail polish was gone.

The big barbecue in the 1960s was still the Stampede event in Mewata Stadium, a football field near the armouries. The ovens were arrayed in the end zone. The various preparation and serving stations were set up there and along one sideline. Food, drink, and dancing went from 1 pm to 6 pm. On stage, bands played all day long. There were demonstrations of square dancing and an occasional comedian.

In many ways, from its inception to the present, the Rotary Barbecue has been the perfect fundraiser. It takes more than the whole club to put one on, and friends, family, and neighbours are regularly dragooned. It's next to impossible not to make friends with the people working all day beside you.

Over the years, members have worried that the club could devolve into a "cheque-writing organization," but Rotary's barbecues are the antidote. Meat cooking, meat carving, bean cooking, bun slicing, bun buttering, food running, beer service, coffee making, cleanup, oven loading — there is not a white-collar job anywhere. It is a service-above-self boot camp.

The people who worked the barbecues tended to do so year after year, even as the number of events rose. They became a community within the Rotary community, with the camaraderie of a travelling circus.

To give an idea of the work, here is an excerpt from a letter by Don Telfer to Barbecue chairman Bill Tynan in 1964:

> On Sunday night we had the Revelstoke trailer and two regular size trucks available at the grounds at 6:30 [pm]. The trucks picked up all the barrels and other equipment and took it out to the steaming area. All the barrels after being steamed were loaded back on to the semi-trailer and the rest of the equipment into the other two trucks. Everything was done and out of the grounds before 9 pm. We also had a Salvation Army truck at 6 pm on Sunday which [picked] up the extra food and took it directly to their hostel. We were informed that good use was made of this food by the Salvation Army.

Another note from the archives describes the feelings of club members about their barbecues. Written by Percy Noel Smith, it reported on a meeting with membership:

> I personally asked, "Do we continue to BBQ or forget it?" At this point the meeting became somewhat out of order. All unanimously said, "Hell yes! What do we have to replace it? What is more fun? What is a bigger gamble? What creates more discussion in the club?" I guess we stay.

(TOP) **GORD WALKER**, president of The Rotary Club of Calgary in 1990, was a long-time volunteer and committee man for the club's barbecues. He is seen here sharpening knives for the carving of roasts.

LOUISE GANT AND CURLY GALBRAITH enjoying a Rotary Stampede Barbecue.

(BOTTOM) **LONG-TIME BARBECUE** volunteer Don Telfer stands ready for action at one of the club's giant barbecue ovens. Roasts of beef were cooked, sliced, and made into sandwiches for the Stampede-time crowds.

For the people working the barbecues, a major change for the better took place in 1976. Lorne Suitor, a commercial plumbing contractor and a major talent at building almost anything, was shown the current state of the art for the club's barbecue and instantly had ideas on how to improve it. The key in his opinion was a ready-packed trailer for hauling the barbecue provisions (the non-refrigerated stuff). Given the go-ahead, Lorne Suitor and Bob Pogue built one together, converting a horse-trailer for the purpose. Bob Pogue gave it a curved roof that accounted for its lasting name: the Chuckwagon.

Years later, when the Chuckwagon was without a means of hauling it, Ron and Gord Graham directed Lorne Suitor to a one-ton, dual-wheel truck with a hoist and large box that was abandoned somewhere in Kananaskis Country. The Grahams had donated it to the Boys and Girls Club and now it sat in a pile of rocks. Lorne Suitor retrieved and repaired the unit. "With a lot of loving care," says Suitor, it was made to haul the Chuckwagon.

Throughout its life, the Chuckwagon was an immense success, called a "saviour" by some. Much of the loading and unloading was a thing of the past. As long as the Chuckwagon was provisioned and the truck gassed up, they were in business.

Keeping the Chuckwagon stocked and controlling the use of the contents became the fiefdom of Mary Tynan. Already an active Rotary Ann, Mary ruled the Chuckwagon with an iron fist. Two members famous for setting up barbecues, trucking the supplies and ovens, and laying out the grounds were Dave MacDonald and Gord Graham.

While the barbecue as a fundraiser was secure and growing, based on private catering jobs, the big Stampede Barbecue went into abeyance for a few years. In 1979, a new kind of Stampede Barbecue showed up. Hammerson Canada Inc., the company that owned the four towers of Bow Valley Square, wanted to put on a huge Stampede Barbecue for the community that occupied its towers. A deal with a commercial restaurant to put on this barbecue fell through at the last moment, and Hammerson asked if Rotary could fill the breach. Things worked out very well: 2,200 paying customers were served and Rotary had the contract for years to come.

Bow Valley Square, however, being right at the heart of downtown, created some problems. To cope with city traffic regulations, one of the giant ovens had to be lifted by crane into a first-storey annex. Ev Mayhood was in charge of the operation.

After that experience, the barbecue moved to the Eau Claire area for several years.

What brought about the next change was the City's wish to find a new use for Mewata Stadium and area. It was to become Shaw Millenium Park with a focus on skateboarding, with an offer that the area could also be the permanent home for Rotary's Stampede Barbecue. Doug Martin was on the Fort Calgary Board at the time, and he proposed a different solution: the barbecue could be moved to Fort Calgary.

Nowadays, the Rotary Stampede Barbecues are known as the "Annual Spectacular." They happen at Fort Calgary, and they are massive. In 2013, the year of Calgary's downtown flood, historic Fort Calgary was on high enough ground to escape the river's overflow. The two Fort Calgary Annual Spectacular Barbecues drew a total of around thirty thousand revelers and netted roughly $400,000 for community service.

• • •

EV MAYHOOD (R), seen here with Richard Copithorne, was chairman of the club's Barbecue Committee for many years.

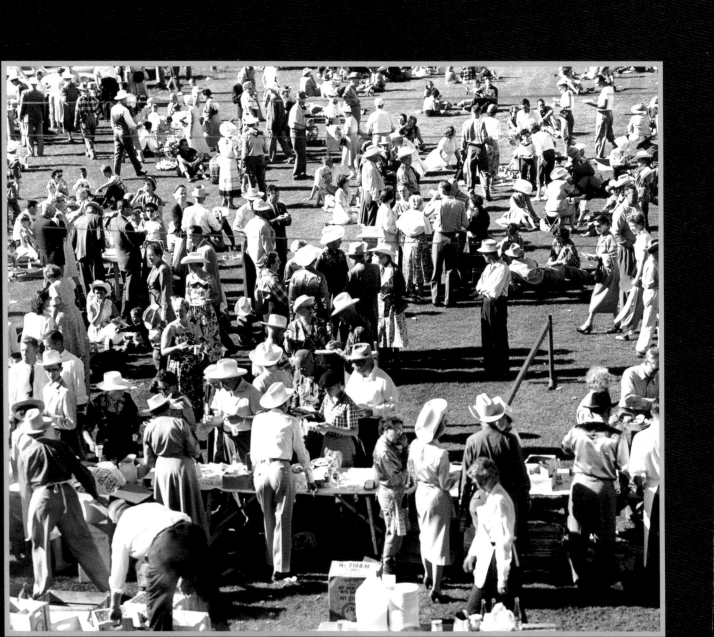

AFTER THE ROTARY CLUB OF CALGARY entered the commercial barbecuing business, it still took on other kinds of fundraisers. In 1959, President Harry Hays got the idea that the club should raffle another house. Memories of the 1944 house raffle caused the board to run the idea past the provincial treasurer and premier. During preparation for this fundraiser it was discovered that Calgary Rotary South had the same plan. The two clubs agreed to work together.

Soon after deciding to go ahead, the Calgary Stampede contacted the clubs. The Stampede had its own house raffle and was concerned the two Rotary Clubs would be selling house raffle tickets at the same time as the Stampede (that is, during Stampede Week). On May 13, Jim Mahaffy met the Stampede's president and general manager and was told the Stampede was "adverse in every way to Rotary selling tickets for their house before midnight July 11." Rotary agreed to the conditions. The fruit of the compromise was $17,115 for the Alberta Crippled Children's Hospital.

A postscript to this story is that Calgary's Rotary South Club eventually made a deal with the Calgary Stampede to sell the Stampede Dream Home. It remains one of that club's top fundraisers.

Also in 1959, The Rotary Club of Calgary went into the Christmas pantomime business. John Stevenson thought it could be profitable. President Jim Mahaffy interviewed the Buskins theatrical group, and the *Aladdin Pantomime* was born. The event was staged at the four-year-old Calgary Jubilee Auditorium.

Buskins came back with *Cinderella* the following year, and the panto drew 12,500 people. The proceeds were divided among five city orphanages. The club could not find a professional company to produce a panto in 1961 but came roaring back in 1962 with *Puss in Boots*.

But the club was still capable of the odd fundraising snafu. So it was with Snider's Water Follies. The story goes that the club's brain trust had a choice between Snider's Water Follies and the Ice Capades. After careful weighing, they chose Water Follies. It was a lovely exhibition of swimming and diving, but people were not much interested. It failed not once but twice. To make the losses feel worse, Ice Capades was a big success. Rotary was offered a chance to sell Ice Capades tickets for fifty cents a ticket.

As Canada's centennial year approached, the club went looking for a suitable gift to the city. A vintage livery stable in Nanton was about to be destroyed, and the club offered to build an exact replica at Calgary's Heritage Park. Don Cushing estimated the cost, and Rotary was good with the plan — but Heritage Park wanted the original stable! The cost of dismantling and rebuilding would be twice as much. The club bit the bullet. By December 13, 1966, Ed Madill reported that the Nanton livery stable, dismantled, was on its way to Calgary. By January 31, it was rebuilt among the other heritage buildings. Club families celebrated the installation of the livery stable on June 26, 1967.

At the start of the 1970s, the club faced an important question. Did it want to become a service organization with extremely large sums of money to distribute or did it want to maintain the comforts of its current size? The occasion was the opportunity to go in with Calgary Philharmonic on an expensive dinner and auction: a society event that might kick them up into a much higher fundraising and donation bracket. The motion could not get a seconder.

What this amounted to was The Rotary Club of Calgary (cohesive, hard-working, traditional) balking on the threshold of the future. If it went for high-flying projects, many feared it would become less hands-on, less friendly.

A related development was the relationship with the United Way. The club had chosen not to donate to the United Way for a couple of years, because it was more at home with its own choice of projects. In 1971, the club gave to a John Howard Halfway House, the Society for Hearing Impaired Children, the Volunteer Bureau, and Boys' Club. It was also paying the transportation costs for a Calgary widow to bring her daughter back to Calgary from Montreal for dialysis. It had sent 112 pairs of ice skates to a Métis community in northern Alberta. Club members wanted personal connection to their community service.

Also affecting the fundraising/service equation, the four Calgary Rotary Clubs had come together to create the Calgary Rotary Clubs Foundation (CRCF). The idea was that the Calgary clubs could create capital within the Foundation. As a club's share in CRCF rose, so too would its distribution amounts. In time, the CRCF disbursement became The Rotary Club of Calgary's largest revenue stream. Part of what made the club's capital share in the CRCF large in a hurry was a $250,000 bequest from Rotarian Matt Brownlee.

● ● ●

ONE WAY OR ANOTHER, The Rotary Club of Calgary kept growing financially through forces that were more economic than internal. In 1976–77, Don Telfer presented club President Vinny Jacques with a great community service opportunity. Don, who would follow Vinny as club

president, was on the board of the Alberta Children's Hospital, and the prospect was to help the hospital build a swimming pool, at an estimated cost of $600,000. Taking this on would represent a major change in a tradition of avoiding multi-year projects. Fundraising would also have to become more professional to meet an obligation of this size. Raffle tickets were not going to cut it anymore.

The board had noticed that fundraising was easier if the worthy recipient touched the hearts of the community. One of the first fundraising events for the pool project was the 1980 Air Canada Children's Hospital Draw. It raised 80 percent more than a similar draw a year before. The club was able to meet its $55,000 payment on the pool project and still have enough left over for other good causes — including underwriting the publication of Rev. Swanny Swanson's memoirs.

ANOTHER FUNDRAISER that came out of the need to raise money for the hospital pool was the celebrity benefit dinner. In 1979–80, when Joe Brager was club president, Bill Kaufmann was put in charge of fundraising. Rotarian Hayden Smith had recently run a "million-dollar dinner" for The Calgary Foundation, and Bill suggested that the club try — if not a million-dollar dinner — a high-priced, black-tie dinner with a celebrity speaker. Bill recalls that the board was not enthusiastic until Dick Yetzer jumped up and announced emphatically that he was behind Bill all the way.

Getting the first speaker proved a problem. Bill Kaufmann describes the hunt: "We tried all sorts of high-profile Americans, but it was the year of the primaries and you could not get anyone." Then he saw a *Time* magazine photo of James Schlesinger. Mr. Schlesinger had been Jimmy Carter's Secretary of Energy and was also

a former head of the CIA, so he had the right kind of credentials, but the key thing about the photograph was that Mr. Schlesinger was in birdwatching garb staring out at a wetland through binoculars. Bill decided to use birding as a lure to bring him north. It worked, and the celebrity dinner had its first celebrity.

All went well until a terrific spring snowstorm hit Calgary on the day of Schlesinger's arrival. By the time he touched down, the storm was over, but Bill had already cancelled the birding expedition. When told there would be no birding that day, Schlesinger, a huge man, grew very stormy. Bill Kaufmann called Dick Yetzer and the expedition was back on.

By nine that night, Yetzer and Schlesinger had not come home. Kaufmann feared they were in a snowy ditch. When Yetzer finally phoned, he explained that they had been birdwatching the whole time. "In the dark?" Bill asked. Yes, said Yetzer; they had been listening for owls.

The Schlesinger dinner sold out, making over $100,000 for the hospital pool. The celebrity dinner became a club annual. In the coming years, the roster of speakers included Zbigniew Brzezinski, Helmut Schmidt, Lord Harold Wilson, General Alexander Haig, Henry Kissinger, Tip O'Neill, Paul Volcker, Peter Hanson, Ted Heath, and Yitzhak Rabin. Over the years, the dinner raised more than $2 million, and the quality of speakers brought to Calgary greatly enhanced the club's stature.

The sod-turning for the Children's Hospital Pool was on June 21, 1983. A year later, the club toured the pool in its final stages. The Children's Hospital had started in 1922 with eighteen beds. Now, it was the only centre serving the long-term health needs of children between Winnipeg and Vancouver. Don Telfer was recognized for his long service on the hospital pool committee.

THE ROTARY CLUB OF CALGARY HOSTED MANY WORLD CELEBRITIES at its fundraising dinners. Dinner chairman John Boyd is seen here with speaker Yitzhak Rabin, 1992.

Fundraising and community service had kicked into another gear. High interest rates meant an enlarged CRCF distribution. In 1985–86, under President Stan Sailer, the club raised $190,000. In 1987–88, Bill Kaufmann's year, fundraising hit $212,000.

The approach during the 1980s was efficient and refined. The club advertised for funding applications in the fall. Those who made the shortlist were asked to come and speak. The preferred areas were projects benefitting young people, seniors, and the handicapped. Another committee dealt with small donations. This allowed the club to be what it had always been: a port in a storm for those whose needs did not fit elsewhere in the social services labyrinth.

On the major-donation side, club funds built classrooms at the Foothills Academy for the Severely Learning Disabled, contributed to a Dementia Centre for the Alzheimer's Society, and gave support to Boys and Girls Club, William Roper Hull Home, Canadian Red Cross, Epilepsy Association, and many others. Small donations bought an electric bed for an arthritic woman, a camera for the Grace Hospital, and provided money to a family that had lost everything in a fire.

THE CLUB'S SEVENTY-FIFTH ANNIVERSARY PROJECT (1989) was to restore the cupola from James Short School and move it from storage to a permanent home at James Short Park.

GEORGE KERBY

The Rotary Club of Calgary has had a long association with the Kerby Centre, devoted to the enhancement of the lives of seniors. The centre was named for Dr. George Kerby, founder of Mount Royal College and Calgary Rotary Club president in 1916–17. One of the Kerby Centre's facilities, the Kerby Rotary Shelter for seniors in crisis, was partly funded by The Rotary Club of Calgary in 1998.

BEARING DOWN ON 2000, the club was on the lookout for a millennium project, a legacy grand enough for the once-in-a-thousand-year occasion. In fact, a project came to them. Duane Schmeekle of Calgary Rotary East was drumming up enthusiasm for Challenger Park among Calgary's clubs. The park would be designed for the fitness needs of people with physical challenges. This future-creating project fit The Rotary Club of Calgary's Vision 2000 concept to a tee.

Walter Haessel represented the club in the Challenger Park planning group. On sixteen acres near the international airport, the idea was to build two baseball diamonds, a track-and-field stadium, a court-sports area, and a barrier-free playground. Because of the expense ($13 million), the variety of funders, and the length of the project, the stakeholder group formed a society for its governance. The Rotary Club of Calgary presented its first $70,000 for Challenger Park to Premier Ralph Klein at a club luncheon.

In 2001–02, under president John Boyd, the club raised its major donation budget to $250,000 per year. An anonymous donor had offered to match the club's major donations. This allowed the club to provide funds to Renfrew Educational Services and Simon House — and still meet its obligation to Challenger Park. Jack Lamarsh and Phil Libin were working behind the scenes to raise another $1.5 million for Challenger. In the end, Calgary's Rotary Clubs contributed enough money to have the park bear Rotary's name: Rotary Challenger Park.

ROTARY CHALLENGER PARK was The Rotary Club of Calgary's millennium legacy project. This athletic park, designed for those with physical challenges, bears the Rotary name because of the many Calgary and regional clubs that invested in its construction. The man with the microphone depicted in this statue is Calgary South Rotarian Ed Whelan.

When Rotary Challenger Park opened in 2003, the club went looking for its next legacy project. In December 2005, The Rotary Club of Calgary and the Rotary Club of Calgary South were invited to join a partnership with the Calgary Flames Foundation. The scope was immense. The partners would fund several medical projects through Reach!, an initiative of Alberta Health Services and the University of Calgary. The rough outline was that the Flames Foundation would give $5 million while the two Rotary Clubs would give $1 million a year for five years. Government would then match the $10 million. Ken King, on behalf of the Flames Foundation, asked for a decision before the 2006 playoffs, just a few months away.

The Reach! projects were a glittering array: a cardio-vascular hypertension centre, a spinal cord repair lab, the first image-guided surgical robot designed and built in Canada — and more. The project would also create Rotary/Flames Park at Ronald McDonald House on the site of Alberta Children's Hospital. In January 2006, The Rotary Club of Calgary confirmed it was in.

The problem with major long-term donations is that, if the economy tanks and investments don't produce, the commitments remain. The aftermath of the 2008 U.S. banking crash unleashed this very scenario.

As the economy worsened, the club's endowment lost value, and the board had to do what it could to cut costs. The club definitely did not want to default on its biggest obligations, such as the Reach! partnership with the Calgary Flames. So, projects were ranked; those at the bottom would likely be cut or have their budgets reduced. In his final report, 2009–10 President Larry Shelley told the club, "We are challenged on our numbers on all fronts. Hopefully, in the next year, we can recover somewhat."

THE MAYHOODS

Ev and Ellen Mayhood were closely associated with The Rotary Club of Calgary for over forty years. Ev was a mainstay of the Barbecue Committee and helped build its profits considerably. The Mayhoods made a substantial fortune in cold storage, and, to celebrate their fiftieth wedding anniversary, Ev and Ellen gave Rotary $50,000, divided between The Rotary Foundation and The Rotary Club of Calgary. This was just the beginning. The couple started the Mayhood Trust that again contributed to both The Rotary Foundation and The Rotary Club of Calgary through the Calgary Rotary Clubs Foundation (CRCF).

Ellen predeceased Ev, and, when Ev died five years later, in 2005, he bequeathed much of his estate to the Mayhood Trust: a sum that may reach $25 million. This amazing bequest has transformed The Rotary Club of Calgary, enabling it to take on community service projects of a formerly unreachable scale. In the first year of the Mayhood bequest, the club's distribution from CRCF rose from $166,000 to $1.7 million. Since then, the annual distribution has ranged from $1.3 million to $2.3 million. Under the terms of the legacy, one half of the Mayhood distribution goes to The Rotary Foundation. That leaves in the order of $600,000 to $800,000 for the local and international work of The Rotary Club of Calgary. In addition, part of the funds sent to The Rotary Foundation come back to the district for international projects. The Mayhoods are two of the most celebrated Calgary Rotarians of all time.

In the tough times that followed, the club's fundraising warhorse, the Rotary Stampede Barbecue (operating under the name Stampede Round-Up) showed its value and muscle once again. In 2009, at the very trough of the economic problems, the fourteenth annual Stampede Round-Up at Fort Calgary sold out with a waiting list.

One person on the board in this period was less worried than the rest about the club's financial dilemma, and that was Eva Friesen. Eva was then, and is now, the CEO of The Calgary Foundation. From this perspective, she knew that what was happening to The Rotary Club of Calgary was happening everywhere. Those awaiting committed charitable donations had much the same point of view as those who owed the money; that is, they would do most anything to avoid default. The usual approach was to stretch the time period of the commitment.

For a brief time the club's cash flow did fall short of the commitment to Reach! but several members of the club stepped to the plate and offered loans at fair interest to bridge the gap.

When the commitment to Reach! was fulfilled, the club moved directly on to its next signature legacy project, one that would celebrate The Rotary Club of Calgary's hundredth anniversary.

A committee drew up a list of six possible projects, but the winner came in the door from another club:

South Calgary. It was Calgary's Greenway Project, and it was as big as they get. The goal of Greenway is to entirely circle the city of Calgary with a 138-kilometre network of parks, natural areas, and paths, including wetland boardwalks.

It did not take The Rotary Club of Calgary long to see that this was the perfect centennial project. It was Calgary; it was healthy; it was family; it was long lasting; and all thirteen Calgary Rotary Clubs were in, plus The Rotary Club of Cochrane and Rotoract. The commitment from the Rotary Clubs was big enough and came early enough that the name would include Rotary. When corporate sponsor Mattamy Homes brought a $5-million contribution, the project became known as the Rotary Mattamy Greenway. Parks Foundation Calgary will be the project's anchor for the many years it will take to complete.

Like the club's other huge projects, Greenway will take a long time, and the club is likely to face occasional struggles to meet the commitment. On the financial side, it is the grand endowment from the Ev Mayhood estate (see "The Mayhoods," p. 95) that allows the club to swing projects this large and to swim across economic rapids when they show up.

But the commitment of club members is what gives the work of fundraising, and community service, its heart: its great big Rotary heart. That part does not change.

THE Show Must Go On

8

THE IDEA THAT FUN CAN BE HAD while doing service is basic to Rotary's value system and personality. The desire to raise funds and enjoy oneself may merge most completely in the putting on of shows. The Rotary Club of Calgary's first variety show for the general public took place in 1917, and, in one form or another, the show has gone on ever since.

IT DOES NOT LOOK ENTIRELY GOOD to present-day values that Rotary's earliest variety shows in Calgary were minstrel shows. White people posing as black people and presenting an evening of wisecracks, music, and slapstick arose in America in the 1830s, solidly within the slave era. After the Civil War, minstrel shows continued, albeit with Black people frequently playing the roles of Black people. The popularity of the minstrel show waned with the appearance of vaudeville in the early twentieth century.

Rotary's 1917 minstrel show was staged at the Grand Theatre where Rotary President Jeff Lydiatt was manager. Forty-eight club members (practically everyone in the club) worked the show, and it turned a nice profit.

In 1923, Rotary International's magazine, *The Rotarian*, ran a piece about minstrel shows as fundraisers. "The vogue of Rotary minstrel shows . . . originated, presumably, from the natural desire for good clean fun and frolic, and from a commendable effort to hasten the flow of silver into the charity coffer."

The article had encouraging things to say about the financial aspects. Words, music, skits, and jokes could all be acquired cheaply. "Excellent negro wigs can be found for $1.24 each and less when secured in quantity lots."

Calgary's Rotary Club had by then produced six successful minstrel shows and was featured in the article. Jeff Lydiatt commented,

> Not only have these entertainments been the medium for raising substantial amounts for community-service work, but the opportunities the rehearsals have afforded for the development of good fellowship have been wonderful, especially for the newer members of the club, whom we invariably press into service.

One of those pressed into service was Lydiatt himself. The first show, directed by Jack Spurr, cast Lydiatt as a soloist. The October 27, 1917, *Calgary Herald* reviewed the event, and Jeff Lydiatt got a plug:

> The make-up was good as one could not see a white mustache, a blonde lock or a red beard anywhere although from what one can remember several of the Rotarians possess such . . . There was a little bit of joking and then Jeff Lydiatt sang "Hallelu-jay," and he must have been watching the professionals on the Grand stage for some time for he sure knew how to do it.
>
> Lon Cavanaugh is some comedian, and he sang "Dat's Harmony" with the aid of the chorus. He did not show off the true qualities of his voice but he was certainly funny.

The time commitment was enormous. Rehearsals went on for six to eight weeks, twice a week at first and then, before opening night, daily. The club's membership included many local business leaders, and they somehow found time to pitch in along with the rest.

The club did reach outside for quality singers but relied on theatre professionals inside the club for its directors and producers. Originally, this was Jeff Lydiatt, but when he departed for Vancouver in 1923, his role was taken over by Maynard Joiner. That is, Joiner became manager of the Grand Theatre and also took over running the Rotary minstrel shows. Others who helped were Jack Bullough, orchestra leader, and Charlie Royal, the vaudevillian who "trained the minstrels." Art McGuire, Walter Davidson, and Hal Morgan worked on the managerial side.

In 1922, the *Calgary Herald* promoted the Rotary Minstrel Show in these words:

> The fact that there is going to be singing and dancing, with all the latest and most up to date jokes and jests, quips and quirks, does not convey much to the average citizen. But the fact that Rotarian Charlie Royal, old-time theatrical man, author and song-writer, is having a lot to do with the general arrangement has convinced many that this Rotary Minstrel Show is really going to be something out of the ordinary . . . In the past the Rotarians have been content to sing a funny song and let it go at that, but with this man Royal it is different. He adds a lot of frills to a song and chorus which will astonish the natives.

The money made was significant. For a three-night run, the minstrel shows yielded $1,500 to $2,000 per year.

When the club was putting on these shows, the era of the minstrel show was in fact over. Like all such variety entertainments, they had been vanquished by professional vaudeville. Why would people want to see a variety show put on by amateurs when they could attend a professional vaudeville show with up-to-the-minute material?

But, in a young and small city like Calgary, that was exactly what made the shows popular: that the players were the local banker, theatre manager, lumber company president, and tailor. In Calgary's downtown, everyone knew everyone, at least by sight, so what a lark it was to see the principal businessmen in black face, dancing and buffooning.

* * *

THOUGH THE CLUB MOVED ON to other methods of fundraising, it was always lured by the exciting early days when the club's minstrel shows were the talk of the town. The next opportunity to try a club-produced variety show came courtesy of the Great Depression. As Donald B. Smith points out in *Calgary's Grand Story*, the deepening depression meant fewer touring professional acts. This brought back the city's interest in local entertainments. In the mid-thirties, Calgary's Rotary Club put on *The Grand Slam of Rotary*, *Sunset Revue*, in which Rotary's singers and dancers performed, bolstered by the Alice Murdoch Dancers. Harry Hutchcroft was the man in charge of the show and received 5 percent of the profits. Harry was not a Rotary member at the time but became one in 1936.

ALMOST EVERY MEMBER of the club was needed onstage to mount the early Grand Theatre minstrel shows.

The *Sunset Revue* ran in 1934 and 1935, turning a profit both times. It is not quite clear whether the 1935 skit called "Chafed and Sunburnt Un-Dated Underwear," was written for the *Sunset Revue*, but it seems likely. At any rate, the skit was such a hit it was repeated at the Rotary District Conference in Banff. Nor was that the end of its life. Chase and Sanborn requested to use the skit at its Chase and Sanborn Dated Coffee Convention. This was a special honour because Chase and Sanborn was also the sponsor of a popular radio variety show and was presumably a connoisseur of both good coffee and good comedy.

What put an end to the *Sunset Review* was not unpopularity but that members tired of selling tickets.

This was not the end of Rotary shows but more of a beginning. Having made the decision not to produce public, commercial shows, Rotary would, in time, start putting on shows for the club's own consumption. That way, the fun and fellowship were retained without the unglamorous flogging of tickets.

In November 1939, rehearsals were under way for a non-profit Rotary show. Harry Hutchcroft was again director, and the work was a musical based on the nursery rhyme *There Was an Old Woman Who Lived in a Shoe*. It was initially prepared for the club's Christmas Family Day, but, before this production, a decision was made to invite three hundred underprivileged kids to take in a dress rehearsal. They were sent home with gifts of food and toys.

That was the first Christmas of World War II, and the all-Rotary cast performed their show a third time at Currie Barracks for the troops.

• • •

ROTARY SHOWS were the entertainment at the Annual President's Ball. Many of them had Broadway show themes — with a Calgary Rotarian twist.

ALL OF THE SHOWS described thus far are ancestors of the modern Calgary Rotary show. The first of these was put on at the inaugural President's Ball in 1953, in Charlie Kennedy's presidential year. In his summation of the year, Charlie reported: "We instituted what we hope will be an annual event, the President's Ball, and all the ladies were of course present at that successful social venture." He made no mention of a floor show, but there was one.

Alice Adams, a member of the original Rotary show cast, had a unique perspective on the first show, having been involved in Rotary's *Sunset Revues* in the 1930s when she was Alice Murdoch of the Alice Murdoch Dancers. She had since married Calgary Rotarian William Adams. Her opinion of the first President's Ball and Rotary show was that the show had been added to "soup up a dull affair."

In the next year's presidential report, Ron Jenkins's only mention of the President's Ball and show was that Ernie Munson, Harry Hays, Art McGuire, and Jack Peach worked on it. The next President's Ball had to be cancelled because it conflicted with the District Conference.

Doris Galbraith was the club's executive secretary during the first years of the Rotary show, and she gives a possible reason why the shows were not well remembered. One year, the show consisted of a Rotary Ann reading the 1953 Kinsey Report: "Sexual Behaviour in the Human Female." Another year (Doris says), "We sat around on the floor of the crystal room. There was a small orchestra playing, and we incorporated them when we needed to. It was really corny."

With time, the show took more formal shape. In 1957, the Rotary show had a name: *Around the World in Eighty Minutes*, a program, and a well-developed script.

THE ROTARY CLUB OF CALGARY inaugurated its President's Ball in 1953, and a floor show of modest proportions accompanied it. In 1957, with *Around the World in Eighty Minutes*, the floor show blossomed into a complex musical entertainment.

The 1959 show was called *Happy Daze with Happy Haze* in honour of President Harry Hays. Merv Cozart was the producer, and his wife Mona Cozart sang the finale: "I'm Just Crazy About Harry." At that year's cast party at Hays Farm, the talent got to watch themselves in a movie that had been shot of the show.

In 1960, the club opted for a Dawson City theme under the title *Klondyke Kapers*. There was both a tall girls chorus line and a men's can-can. Men dressed up as women is one of the recurrent themes of Rotary shows, and it was seldom a pretty sight. And who could ever forget Mona Cozart's heartbreaking "My Baby Has Gone Down the Plug Hole?"

In 1961, Rotary show stalwart Merv Cozart was president and *The Rotary Show Boat* was performed.

There was a consistent naming style to the acts: "The Casino Cuties," "The Levee Loafers," "The Dixie Darlings," "The Tennessee Tambourines," and "The Bayou Bouncers" (more male dancers in drag, one fears).

There was an Irish night in 1962. The lights came up on a leprechaun leaning on a lamppost with an empty whisky bottle in his hand. (Stereotypes were not avoided in Rotary shows but rather encouraged.)

The 1964 show was in honour of the club's Golden Anniversary. It was divided into five acts dedicated to the songs and dances of each of the club's five decades: Ziegfeld Girls; a Charlie Chaplin impersonator; Vinnie Jacques as a ringlet-ed chiffon-ed Shirley Temple; Harry Hays, Ward Tennis, and Charlie Kennedy as three-quarters of the musical group "The Beagles." Women in the audience were encouraged to scream and swoon.

The year 1969 was particularly exciting for the club's show people. The Rotary show that year was attended by Montana lumberman Tiny Ough, who liked it so much he decided he would pay to have it re-staged in his hometown of Livingston, Montana. That year, Mr. Ough was president of Livingston's Rotary Club. The cast was flown from Calgary to Livingston on a Pacific Western charter and put up in local hotels. Clarese Sailer was a cast member and has always felt guilty that the citizens of Livingston "had to pay" to watch them.

Sometimes, the Rotary show-people were employed for off-stage antics. Such was the case in September 1969 when the club was putting on a barbecue for a Canadian Chartered Accountants convention. The convention was in Banff, and the barbecue was at Calgary's Heritage Park. The conventioneers travelled by train from Banff to the barbecue, and there were various Rotary western role-players aboard. One was a western parson who was busy saving sinners. Then there was Mona Cozart as a frontier "Madam" with a few soiled doves. One such dove was Clarese Sailer, wearing her can-can outfit from the Rotary show.

At Morley, the train halted. Stoney Natives in full war paint rode in on the train and kidnapped the soiled doves. As Clarese was borne away across the pommel of a Native's horse, she had to beg the man to let her down so the train did not leave without her.

The ideas for Rotary shows were often drawn from show business. They often combined a well-known commercial show with Rotary content. The 1978 offering was titled *Quo Vadis*, with the subtitle "Where the hell are we if we ain't in Rome?" The program was made to look like an Air Canada ticket, only the airline name was "Air Chaos." The storyline: "A fanciful tale of how the Calgary Rotary show might have got to the RI in Italy — if it had been invited."

The director of many Rotary shows in the 1970s was Joe Brager, and everyone agreed he did a fine job. But when Frank McKitrick, a virtuoso piano player and organist, took over in the 1980s, there was also general agreement that the shows went from "girls and boys having a good time," as Stan Sailer put it, to a certain degree of professionalism.

The 1983 Rotary show *Over There* was based on another upcoming Rotary International conference in England. Alongside favourite English show tunes, there was a demonstration of Ye Olde English Morris Dancing.

Show names were often derived from the current president's name. For example, in 1968, the show had a nautical theme and was titled *Skip Ahoy*, based on President Owen Funnell's Rotary nickname, "Skipper."

In 1987–88, Bill Kaufmann's presidential year, the show was *Tales of Kaufmann*. In the show, a sleeping beauty (Clarese Sailer) was to be awakened by a kiss from the prince (Bill Kaufmann). On the night of the show, Clarese put honey on her lips ("the creamy kind, really sticky"). It was a major surprise for Kaufmann who claimed he "could not disengage."

The 1995 Rotary show, *Camp Toomsawaga*, was at the expense of president Garth Toombs. "The director of *Camp Toomsawaga* is an Ebenezer Scrooge type of dictator who changes his ways only after being visited by the Ghost of Summer Past and the Ghost of Summer Yet to Come." Here's a sample of the script:

Camp director: Okay, those who wish to go swimming may go swimming — but remember, no running, no drowning, and no discoloring the lake.

All campers drop clothes and are wearing swim attire, and run to lake.

(*The Tall Girls Dance Line Presents: "Yellow Polka Dot Bikini."*)

One of the swimmers: Where's the lifeguard?

The lifeguard comes running with a dreamy look on his face.

Lifeguard: I've been getting private lessons from the swimming instructor.

Swimming instructor: Yeah, I just taught him the breaststroke! C'mon big boy, and I'll teach you the crawl.

• • •

ROTARY SHOW TITLES often punned on the name of the current president. *Tales of Kaufmann* was presented in 1987–88, Bill Kaufmann's presidential year.

FRANK MCKITRICK

Frank McKitrick has been all things musical to The Rotary Club of Calgary. As piano accompanist at club luncheons, he is justly famous for his sophisticated arrangements — including a high-speed version of "O Canada" — and being able to play with his back to the keyboard (doing bass bumps with his bum). He directed and assisted many Rotary shows. Beyond Rotary, his career included teaching drama at Winston Churchill High School and serving as organist at Knox United Church. Frank grew up in North Battleford, Saskatchewan. His home was half a block away from that of Joan Anderson (better known to the world as Joni Mitchell). In grade four, Frank and Joan had desks in the same classroom. Frank's recollection of Joni is that she was more interested in art than music at the time. Joni's recollection is that Frank was the reason she took piano lessons.

FRANK MCKITRICK at the keyboard with Irene Besse.

As with the Rotary barbecues, the crowd of volunteers who put on Rotary shows was built around a stable core of veterans: Rotarians with serious show business skills. Dancers at the Rotary show were directed by Alice Adams and Jean Simpson (sisters) for many years. Bev White was in charge of music. Ola MacNutt and later Mary Tynan directed the chorus. Geoff Naylor was in charge of sets. Wilda Graves and Marj Jacques were stalwarts in costume design and production. Pat Cushing did makeup. Ron Graham built the stage and sets. John Shipley was perennial master of ceremonies. Harry Hays and Charlie Kennedy could be called on for most anything. In later years, that core would include Joe Brager, Frank McKitrick, and the Averys (Randy and, later, Bill).

The Livingston, Montana, trip was one of several times the Rotary show went on the road. The show was performed at Rotary District Conferences in Lethbridge, Swift Current, Edmonton, Banff, and Calgary. As of 1987, the Rotary show, including road shows, had been performed fifty times in thirty-five years.

All good things come to an end, they say, and for a time it appeared the Rotary show was going to end with the old millennium. Ron Robertson and Bill Avery appeared before the board in 2001 to report that they only had twenty in the chorus and ten in the tall girls chorus line. They had decided to fill the gaps with performers from the Young Canadians and, for material, to borrow from the Calgary Stampede Grandstand Show that Bill Avery was also directing.

RANDY AND BILL AVERY

Randy Avery, originally of New York, moved to Canada in the 1960s to become executive producer of the Calgary Stampede Grandstand Show. He joined The Rotary Club of Calgary soon after his arrival. It was under Randy's leadership that the Young Canadians performing group was developed and became a featured attraction at the Grandstand Show. Bill Avery took over from his father as CEO of the Grandstand Show in 1987. Both men have contributed to the history and professionalism of the Rotary show.

The upshot was that the club's Rotary show could not go on in this fashion. Another part of the problem was that dinner dances were not as popular with younger members. So the club moved on — for a while.

What happened over the next several years was that the club began to miss its Rotary show. It had been fun, and its absence left a significant hole in the Rotary calendar. In 2006, the Rotary show was revived on a smaller scale.

And it has kept on going. In 2013, Bill Avery, back in the directorial saddle, not only put on a Rotary show in conjunction with the President's Ball but realized a profit of $7,000.

• • •

WHEN JEFF LYDIATT TOLD *The Rotarian*, in 1923, that rehearsing a variety show "afforded a good opportunity for fellowship," it was considerable understatement. Though far from easy to do, the mounting of a variety show has, packed within it, countless laughs and opportunities to discover new talents and depths in people you thought you knew. When Rotary members and Rotary Anns reminisce about forty-year-old shows, it is as vivid to them as yesterday, and this is another of the gifts that Rotary gives to those who immerse themselves deeply in it: that you will have memorable fun; that you will have friends for all time; that your life will not lack in laughter.

As Bugs Bunny said, "On with the show! This is it!"

Good FOR the Club 9
Women in Rotary

9

WHAT WOULD MEN BE WITHOUT WOMEN?
Scarce, sir — mighty scarce.

—Mark Twain

THIS BOOK CELEBRATES ONE HUNDRED YEARS OF The Rotary Club of Calgary. One of the Honorary members of the club, Dr. Marmie Hess, is also nearing one hundred. Her father, Fred Hess, joined Calgary Rotary in 1915. Marmie was born a year later. Of her life, she says, "I was a single child. Rotary has meant everything to me. It has connected through my whole life."

What this statement proves is that it has always been possible for a woman in a Rotary family to have a close connection with Calgary's Rotary Club. This is not meant to discount the importance of the inclusion of women in Rotary as full members, but it does underline that women have always been part of, and of key importance to, Calgary's original Rotary Club.

• • •

THE EARLY HISTORY OF Calgary's first Rotary Club does come across as an all-male affair, perhaps because wives did not go to Tuesday luncheons in the earliest days. In December 1921, the board decided that, on special occasions, wives would be invited to lunch. Also in its early days, the club had a father-and-son lunch. This soon became a father-and-daughter-and-son lunch, when Fred Hess and Jim Davidson insisted on being able to bring their daughters as well.

Most histories of Rotary mention that Rotary wives were called "Rotary Anns," a practice that began in 1914 on a train taking Rotarians to the convention in Houston. There was just one wife aboard, and her name was Ann Brunier. The Rotarians on the train started calling her "Rotary Ann." When the Bruniers got to Houston, they met Guy and Ann Gundaker from Philadelphia, and Mrs. Gundaker became "Rotary Ann" too. From there it spread to include all Rotary wives.

Or did it? The first written mention of Rotary Anns in The Rotary Club of Calgary board minutes does not appear until the end of 1947–48, when James Fowler used the term in his outgoing president's report. Elsewhere, the wives of club members were referred to reliably as "the ladies." This does not mean the term was never used in the club; it might have been. But the sparsity of its use suggests that Rotary Ann was more of an American usage that only caught on in Calgary in the late forties and fifties.

• • •

DR. MARMIE HESS and Alberta's Lieutenant Governor, Donald S. Ethell, at Remembrance Day ceremony, 2013. Dr. Hess is an Honorary Member of The Rotary Club of Calgary and has had a lifelong association with the club. Her father, Fred Hess, joined Calgary's first Rotary Club in 1915.

A TOUGH ACT TO FOLLOW

The first executive secretary of The Rotary Club of Calgary was Verena "Jack" Williams. Jack's husband was the popular Rotarian James Williams. Rotarians appreciate good singing, and Jim Williams had a beautiful baritone voice He was a featured soloist in the early minstrel shows. But a ruptured appendix killed him in his prime and left his wife, Jack, a widow with three children. Jack had been farm-raised in Ontario; she was capable, self-reliant, and determined to earn her keep. Her parents sold their farm and moved to Calgary to help with the care of the children, and Jack went back to work. She started with Calgary's Rotary Club as part-time secretary in 1921, and was made full-time a bit later. In total, Jack Williams was the club's secretary for twenty-five years. She retired in 1945, a year after her marriage to club founder-member Doug Howland, as they were moving to Vancouver. She was by then so synonymous with the club, members could scarcely imagine it without her. When the club said its farewell, the speech in her honour ended, "Jack was the best Rotarian of us all."

This was a very hard act to follow, but Mrs. Merrill Huntley did so for seven years. In 1952, she was succeeded by Doris Mercer, who would become Mrs. Doris Galbraith. This is a good story best told by Doris herself. Doris had been working at the Palliser Hotel, first in the basement on the telephone switchboard and eventually at the front desk. The Rotary office was in the Palliser Hotel, and, when their executive-secretary job came open, Doris got it — and loved it.

As for how this led to her marriage to Curly Galbraith, Doris claims that Curly "was the only eligible bachelor in the club." When RI Conference was in Seattle, the club asked Doris to attend. Curly was taking his car and said he would drive her. Charlie Kennedy and Harry Hays, the club's reigning wits, bet that, if Curly drove Doris to Seattle, they would marry within a year. And so it transpired. After five years of working for the club, Doris gave up her job and became Mrs. Galbraith.

Helen Terry took over as executive secretary from 1957 until 1965. Then came Audrey Farnsworth (1966–82) and Mrs. Daphne Wilson (1983–87). Sandra Elliott became executive secretary in 1988 and served until 2008. Tina Jarrett was next. Somewhere along the line, the job title was changed to office manager. The current office manager, Jo-Ann Clarke, started with the club in 2011.

JO-ANN CLARKE
(seen here with past president Gord Walker) is office manager of The Rotary Club of Calgary. Jo-Ann is the latest in a long and illustrious line of women who have kept the club between the sidelines.

ONE OF THE CLUB'S HISTORICAL ANECDOTES, or jokes, is that it took more than thirty years to initiate a ladies' night. This appears not to be so. In January 1926, a "Ladies meeting" is mentioned. The "ladies of the club are to be in charge" and it is to "take the form of a dinner and dance." A year later, a similar function, this time in February, is called "Ladies' night." Ladies' nights and ladies' luncheons continued until the depression cut them off — an exception being when Doug Howland returned from Asia. The full restoration of ladies' nights in 1936 (one including a fashion show) was a sign that the economic gloom was lifting.

What changed the role of women in the club was the work of Rotary wives during World War II. In the fall of 1939, the wives formed what was called a "Ladies Red Cross Unit." Their purpose was to knit and sew articles useful to soldiers at war. The club was asked to support buying supplies necessary to this work, and it consented. The women's group soon changed its name to Ladies Red Cross Auxiliary.

The amount of work done by this group was astonishing. From the start, they were making heavy bathrobes and bandages of all kinds. In December 1939, a sentence appears in the board minutes with a different tone than anything said about women to date: "What can we do to prove to the ladies that we are behind them in this real effort they are making?"

The main things the ladies asked for were new sewing machines, as the old ones wore out (including a switch from treadle to electric), and space to work in. The Rotarians found space in the Burns Building and later in the Bank of Canada Building. In 1941–42, the Ladies Red Cross Auxiliary, under president Mrs. Fred Weir, turned in to the Red Cross 2,580 sewn articles, 200 seaman's coats, and 246 knitted articles.

What this meant, in part, was that the club wives were organized, and they did not stop being organized when the war ended. (For that matter, they did not stop sewing and knitting for those in need, either.) It might be too bold to say that the work of the Ladies Red Cross Auxiliary single-handedly changed the relationship between club men and the group of club women, but it certainly pushed it in the direction of change.

However it came about, a perceptible difference existed in the way The Rotary Club of Calgary spoke about wives of club members before, during, and after the war.

At the end of 1945–46, outgoing President Bill Knights included club wives in his report:

> The ladies enjoyed a happy season of bowling, held several luncheons, completed considerable work in their Red Cross group, and completely swamped the men in the bowling windup. We closed a season of family association with a picnic, which will be long remembered by the large group that attended. The ladies also made the magnificent contribution of $2,500 toward our Boys' Town work.

The next outgoing president's report was the one in which James Fowler referred to the women as Rotary Anns. The Anns had held luncheons, teas, and a fashion show that year, and they had bowled. They were continuing with their Red Cross work and were selling coupons for a circus. They had added visiting at the Colonel Belcher to their service work.

Having earned great respect for their Red Cross war work, and now organized as Rotary Anns, the women of the club did not wait for invitations but staged events of their own (teas, fashion shows, dinners, parties) to which the men were invited. They had their own sports program

that often included mixed contests against the men. They did their own fundraising. They were definitely still supporting the work of their Rotary husbands, but some of the old patriarchy was gone.

When the club began its President's Ball and Rotary shows, the women of the club were on stage and working at every level. As the shows became more sophisticated, women appeared as dancers, group singers, and soloists. They designed and sewed costumes. They directed the chorus and choreography; wrote scripts. When the club began its barbecues in the 1950s, the women were again fully involved. Rotary barbecues were family work bees. When giving his outgoing presidential report in 1960, James Mahaffy said,

> I wonder how many of us have ever stopped to think of the tremendous share of our Rotary activities which is borne by our wives. The Rotary Anns are certainly a tower of strength to this Calgary club and our sincere thanks go to their President, Hilda Pinnell, her executive and her entire membership.

When Doris Galbraith talks about her experience as a Rotary Ann and as president of that organization ("We all took our turn."), she remembers the events and the fundraising ("We bought a dialysis chair."), but there is a sense that the question of what the women were doing as opposed to the men is a bit beside the point. They were doing the work of Rotary, together; and they were doing the play of Rotary too. Bowling, ping-pong, dinner dances; fellowship.

When the issue of full membership for women arose throughout the Rotary world, largely in the 1980s, the discussion was not spurred by a desire for membership among Rotary Anns. Asking this question of women who were Rotary Anns and Rotary daughters usually elicits a response that full membership was not sought because women already felt like equals in Rotary. Many Rotary Anns liked having their own club and preferred it to any notion of mixing with the men in theirs.

In the 1980s, The Rotary Club of Calgary circulated a questionnaire to its members and their wives asking whether they were in favour of or against full membership for women. More women than men were against female membership at that time.

• • •

VERNEIL MARTIN'S
AMONG FRIENDS

The Rotary Club of Calgary has two cookbooks in its history. In 1963, Curly Galbraith and Jim Fetterly suggested a Rotary barbecue cookbook as a fundraiser. Rotary wives contributed recipes, a modest book was published, and some money was made over several years.

In 1986, Verneil Martin planned something much larger: a cookbook that would raise money for Rotary International's PolioPlus campaign (aimed at eradicating polio worldwide). Verneil took the project to the District 536 Governor (her husband, Doug Martin) who agreed to finance it. But Rotary International was not interested. Even Rotarians in Calgary told her to drop the idea. This only spurred Verneil on. She registered the title, *Among Friends*. She canvassed the District for recipes.

Among Friends was an instant bestseller. In its first two years, it sold twenty thousand copies and raised $800,000 for PolioPlus. The success and earning power of the cookbook did not stop there. Eventually, *Among Friends* raised over $1 million, providing eighty million immunization shots.

Verneil Martin has been honoured many times. She received six Paul Harris Fellowships and was made a Benefactor of Rotary International. In 1991, she said she hoped to do two more cookbooks while she was able. She had a disease that could render her blind at any time. If that is not service above self, it is hard imagine what could be.

(TOP) **VERNEIL MARTIN,** seen here with husband Doug Martin (left) and Dave Johnston, raised more than $1 million for PolioPlus with her *Among Friends* cookbook.

THE CLUB'S FIRST COOKBOOK was *The Stampede Barbecue,* published in 1963.

LIKE ROTARY CLUBS ALMOST EVERYWHERE, The Rotary Club of Calgary was divided on the question of female membership. Those with the longest experience tended to feel that female membership was not needed. The club worked well without it. But as many members who lived through the change say today, it was not really a matter of what the club wanted. The world was changing. Men and women were equals in the workplace. Well-educated women were rising to positions of leadership in business. How could a business club like Rotary stay representative of the business community without women as members?

The male-only wording of the Rotary constitution was becoming more and more out of date, and, to stay current and relevant, Rotary did need to become a club for people, not just men.

The movement toward female membership is well documented. It began in California, where a court ruled Rotary's men-only status illegal. When the California Supreme Court upheld the ruling, Rotary appealed. A similar legal process worked its way through Canadian courts. All over the Rotary world, clubs debated it, sometimes acrimoniously. This is already an over-simplification, but a fuller account may not add much. In January 1989, at a meeting of the Council on Legislation of Rotary International, in Singapore (attended by Curly Galbraith), a motion was presented to remove the word "male" from all club documents and replace it with "person." A 74 percent majority of those present voted for this change.

It was left to individual clubs to opt in or opt out, and Calgary Rotary stayed with the status quo for two more years. In February 1991, Calgary philanthropist and former Rotary Ann, Martha Cohen, was asked to be

PAUL HARRIS'S NIECE, NAN WALKER JENSEN (left) and Calgary philanthropist Martha Cohen were offered honourary memberships in The Rotary Club of Calgary in 1991. Their acceptance officially opened club membership to women.

an Honourary Member of The Rotary Club of Calgary, as was Nan Jensen, Paul Harris's niece. Gord Walker is credited with the idea of asking these two women, both of whom brought with them such enormous respect, to be the first two female members of The Rotary Club of Calgary. He knew no one would voice an objection to either of these honourary members — and that the women who joined as regular members thereafter would have their way paved before them.

No doubt there are some Rotary elders somewhere who believe the old system made for better fellowship or better family service work, but for the majority of Rotarians, the entry of women into the clubs was positive. Predicted negative results did not happen. Unexpected positive changes did. For example, a problem for many Rotary Clubs, including Calgary's, has been a rising average age and a general difficulty in attracting younger members. Though there has not been a flood of

women members into the Calgary Rotary Club (the figure stands at about 8 percent of membership), the women who do join are usually younger than the average age. When male work associates are attracted to Rotary by Rotarian female co-workers, these too tend to be younger. Studies of the Rotary world show that women Rotarians, on average, shoulder more service work than their male counterparts.

If there is a significant loss associated with the entry of women into Calgary Rotary, it is the disappearance of the Rotary Anns organization. The process began with a change of name. If the women of Rotary were full members, and their partners, if male, wanted to be associated with the club, the place for them was in the Rotary Anns — but the name did not fit very well. Rotary Anns was changed to Rotary Partners. The Partners organization continued for more than a decade, but gradually the numbers decreased, and the Partners organization disbanded.

This was not without impact. In 1973, in a letter of advice to a new Rotary Club in Alberta, Curly Galbraith wrote: "We in the Calgary Club feel that the success of our club is due to a very large extent to the support which we receive from our ladies, and I feel sure that all clubs would be strengthened if the wives were actively involved in Rotary activities."

That same year, Rotary Ann President Evelyn Buckley ended a talk to a West Calgary Rotary luncheon with these words: "By making more use of this potential — wife power — you could actually double your working power. Please don't underestimate our willingness or ability to help."

The Rotary Anns were a powerful force of service within Rotary Clubs. Take all that work, energy, and inventiveness away and something powerful had to be lost. Some Rotary spouses did become full Rotary members, but they were a minority. Most remained in the Rotary Ann category, and some of their service was simply lost when Rotary Partners disbanded.

But something else should be mentioned. It was not only the move to full membership for women that caused this. As has been often the case with great changes at Rotary, it was a matter of history. Over the last sixty years of Rotary, the number of stay-at-home housewives went from the majority to the minority — and quite a small minority. Rotary Anns were at their most powerful when they did not have jobs outside the home. They were no doubt busy at home, but they were able to make the time to help Rotary. When they had their own careers, Rotary Partners had their own service obligations stemming from those careers.

As for the female members of Rotary, as their numbers have risen, so too has their power. All over the Rotary world, women have become club presidents and District governors. In 2013–14, part of the celebration of The Rotary Club of

By 1994, the average age at The Rotary Club of Calgary was above seventy; few younger people were joining. There was a gender imbalance and a lack of ethnic diversity. A Vision 2000 report generated these ideas:

1. Organizations exist to enable ordinary people to do extraordinary things.
2. The future is not some place we are going but someplace we are creating.
3. Paths are not found but made, and making them changes the maker and the destination.
4. You can't expect different results if you continue to do the same things.

Club members got to work on change, and, as 2000 approached, one-third of the club was made up of new members. The percentage of women was far from 50 percent but growing.

Calgary's centennial is the election of its first female president: Eva Friesen.

Eva is a career CEO. She has been CEO of the YWCA in Yellowknife and Calgary, and she has been CEO of the Calgary Health Trust. Since 2005, she has been CEO of The Calgary Foundation. She is a powerful leader. Asked if female membership was much of an issue when she first joined Rotary (at the Calgary Centennial Club in the early nineties), she says not at all. Whatever was involved in making the choice in favour of full membership for women, Rotary got on with their normal business quickly thereafter. There was a similar ease when, after taking a parenting break, Eva joined again, this time at the Calgary downtown club.

As to where Eva would like to take The Rotary Club of Calgary, she wants it to be as attractive to young people as it was in Chicago when Paul Harris and his group started the movement. They were men in their thirties. Every club grows older and must find a way to refresh itself, she says. The aging happens because people enjoy Rotary so much they want to continue. Wise, older people at the podium are wonderful, but the young do not see themselves in that picture, says Eva, and if they cannot see themselves in the picture, they are unlikely to join. With that in mind, Eva chose thirty-year-old Chris Harper to be secretary to her presidency, and all agree he did a good job.

As to why Eva Friesen agreed to be president of The Rotary Club of Calgary, she gives three reasons. First, it was Larry Shelley and Bruce Fenwick who asked her, and, "They are men you can't say no to." Her main reluctance was that she did not want to take time away from her two daughters, and Bruce Fenwick told her that, at fifteen and seventeen, the ages they would be in her presidential year, they were unlikely to want to spend a lot of time with their mother, anyway. Eva laughingly admits this is true. The third reason is the club's centennial. To have the first female president in The Rotary Club of Calgary's history preside over its centennial year "is good for the club."

• • •

Taking Action Around THE World

10

"Rotary is a miniature model of a world at peace."

— Paul Harris

A PERSON HAS ONLY TO LOOK at the 1920s and 1930s Asian extension work of James Wheeler Davidson and Doug Howland to know that Rotary International and The Rotary Club of Calgary have always been interested in the greater world.

THOUGH ROTARY HAS ALWAYS RESPONDED to world events, especially international disasters, there was a considerable shift in the Rotary approach to international service after World War II. The extension work done between the wars by Wheeler and Howland was part of a Rotary dream of international peace and balance: a hope that Rotary as a movement could promote world understanding and peace. But World War II happened anyway, and, before that war was over, Rotary was already at work on a new international plan.

During World War II, several Rotarians contributed to the writing of the United Nations charter and the founding of that institution in 1945. Ever since that time, RI and particularly The Rotary Foundation have invested heavily in international work, and clubs and districts were encouraged to do likewise.

The Rotary Club of Calgary was not in the vanguard of Rotary's strong move toward international involvement. At the end of World War II, Alberta was dealing with a housing shortage, a job shortage, and serious population loss. Then, out of the blue, came the 1947 oil strike at Leduc. This discovery unlocked a secret about Alberta's geology that led to many more strikes and oil fields. This industrial awakening led to provincial wealth that very few could have predicted.

The post-war Alberta oil boom was a starting gun for national and multinational oil companies to come to Alberta. They set up shop here and pushed the pace of provincial development. Calgary was, and is, the office headquarters of the Canadian oil industry. In the 1970s, when OPEC choked supply and pushed up the world oil price, Alberta's Premier Peter Lougheed began to lobby the federal government to allow the Alberta oil price to rise too. Eventually, Premier Lougheed succeeded in attaining the world price for Alberta oil, and Calgary boomed.

When Calgary became an economic player on the world stage, The Rotary Club of Calgary took on a great deal more international work. But, before we go into that story, a quick review of the club's history of international service is in order.

●   ●   ●

THE ROTARY CLUB OF CALGARY'S first international project came in 1917, the same year that the International Association of Rotary Clubs created an endowment for international work. (In 1928, this endowment was renamed The Rotary Foundation.)

The Calgary club's 1917 project was Boots for Belgium. Calgary Rotarians collected ten thousand pairs of wearable boots and sent them to Europe. Not bad for a city of sixty-five thousand. Future club president Lon Cavanaugh, a large man, was one of those going door to door. After hearing his spiel, an older woman looked him up and down and said that she might have some boots around the place, but she doubted any would fit him.

The financial constraints of the 1920s and 1930s prevented much in the way of international donations, but the club still made two important strides at that time. In the 1920s and '30s, prominent Calgary Rotarians James Wheeler Davidson and Doug Howland combined to found forty-seven Rotary Clubs in nineteen countries, mostly in Asia: that was the first stride. The second was helping in the creation of the Waterton-Glacier International Peace Park in the early 1930s.

In the latter stages of World War II, Calgary Rotarians assisted areas badly hit by the war. The club contributed funds to the Docklands Settlement in London and to the relief of Greece. After the war, when Britain was beset

(LEFT) **THE PARCELS FOR BRITAIN CAMPAIGN** to relieve flood-ravaged Britain after the war was The Rotary Club of Calgary's biggest community service campaign to date. Most of the parcels were packaged for shipping in Jenkins' Groceteria. Club member Ron Jenkins took over the groceteria business in 1945 and expanded it to include forty-eight stores. (RIGHT) **AN INTERNATIONAL PROJECT** undertaken by The Rotary Club of Calgary in the 1960s involved the purchase of this van for Arogyavaram Eye Hospital in Sompeta, India.

by floods, Calgary's Rotary Club put together its biggest drive ever: Parcels for Britain. The club sorted, packed, and shipped parcels, with much of that work being done in Jenkins' Groceteria. Eight thousand pounds of clothing were sent to Britain.

When Rotary's founder Paul Harris died in 1947, contributions poured in to Rotary International. These donations became the Paul Harris Memorial Fund, which helped The Rotary Foundation take on international work. Rotary Clubs like Calgary's were asked by Rotary International to subscribe to the Paul Harris Memorial Fund, and the Calgary club did so.

The Rotary Club of Calgary's international work was given a further boost when RI created World Community Service (WCS), a system linking Rotary Clubs in need of project funds with Rotary Clubs that had money to give. In 1968, WCS offered The Rotary Club of Calgary two projects in India. As a result, the club bought educational play equipment for a children's park in Hyderabad and a medical van for schools in Madras. Over the next two

decades, the club contributed to many WCS projects: digging artesian wells in the Philippines, an eyesight unit in Bangladesh, a hospital in St. Lucia, an agricultural school in Darjeeling, cultivating equipment for seniors in Uruguay, a water and sewage project in Lima, a hospital in Guatemala City, and a health centre in Belize.

Another way the club invested in international work was by awarding Paul Harris Fellowships to recognize club members and also non-Rotarians for outstanding contributions to society. The system of Paul Harris Fellowships was launched in 1957. By investing $1,000 in The Rotary Foundation (to support international work) a club was able to purchase one Paul Harris Fellowship, which it could then bestow on whomever it felt deserved the honour. The first members of The Rotary Club of Calgary to become Paul Harris Fellows were Dave Black, Maurice Brown, Matt Brownlee, Bill Knights, Curly Galbraith, Fred McKinnon, Swanny Swanson, Fred Kennedy, Alf Middleton, Ron Graham, and Sam Coultis.

● ● ●

WATERTON-GLACIER INTERNATIONAL PEACE PARK ASSEMBLY

The Rotary Club of Calgary's longest international commitment is the Waterton-Glacier International Peace Park. In 1930, club members participated in an international goodwill meeting at Waterton Lakes, attended by southern Alberta and Montana Rotary Clubs. From this meeting came the idea of turning Waterton Lakes National Park and Glacier National Park into Waterton-Glacier International Peace Park. Joseph Low of the Cardston Rotary Club and Frank Freeze of Calgary had a hand in this, and the dedication ceremony took place on June 18, 1932. Both Prime Minister R. B. Bennett and President Hoover sent messages.

Ever since that year, an annual Rotary celebration of the peace park has alternated between Waterton and Glacier locations. To this day, Rotary governs the Waterton-Glacier Peace Park Association, and Canadian and American Rotary Clubs assemble on a September weekend to recite this pledge: "In the name of God we will not take up arms against each other. We will work for peace, maintain liberty, strive for freedom, and demand equal opportunities for all mankind. May the long existing peace between our two nations stimulate other people to follow this example."

IN 1985, Rotary International launched its largest-ever global initiative: PolioPlus. The amazingly ambitious goal was the complete eradication of this crippling and potentially fatal disease. PolioPlus began its work in Paraguay, Turkey, and Sudan. Ten million people in those countries were to receive their first dose of polio vaccine. Plans had been approved for ten more programs that would immunize seventy million children.

The Rotary Club of Calgary response to PolioPlus was positive and dramatic, in part because so many in the club had lived through the polio epidemic of 1949–54, which left eleven thousand Canadians paralyzed. The club's Edworthy family had a personal connection. Bonnie Edworthy had contracted the disease in 1953 when she and George were farming in northern BC. In support of PolioPlus, Bonnie spoke to the Calgary club of her experience. In 1987–88, the donation to PolioPlus by Rotary Club of Calgary members was $185,000.

At the RI Convention in the spring of 1988, it was announced that PolioPlus was $100 million over target, making it the most successful drive in Rotary history. By 2005, the number of countries endemic for polio was reduced to four. Between 1985 and 2005, the number of new polio cases fell by 99 percent.

Among Calgary's contributions to PolioPlus, two stand out: Verneil Martin's amazing fundraising effort (over $1 million raised for the cause by her cookbook *Among Friends*) and the contribution of Connaught Laboratories. Rotary Club of Calgary member Bill Cochrane was president of Connaught Laboratories in 1996. At the RI Convention in Calgary that year, he announced that Connaught Laboratories, which had run important field trials of Salk vaccine in the 1950s, was contributing thousands of doses of vaccine to the polio fight. CP Air offered to carry the vaccine doses to Manilla at no cost.

· · ·

THOUGH THE CLUB certainly upped its international game in the seventies and eighties, not everyone felt it was enough. The club's budget for world community service had been $5,000 for some time. In 1991–92, President Terry McMahon and his board decided that number was behind the times. Their feeling was that the club had been playing supporting roles rather than undertaking international projects of its own. John Bertagnolli, chairman of the World Community Service Committee, was put in charge of changing things.

In November 1991, board member Ron Middleton made a game-changing suggestion. The club's major donations budget had never been used for international work. What Ron suggested was that part of that budget be dedicated to international projects. The initial amount was set at $10,000. The club began considering international proposals, large and small, much as it did with its domestic community service work.

In the fall of 1993, the international proposals included projects in the Himalayas and in Kwe Kwe, Zimbabwe. The club decided to give $20,000 to a Himalayan rural health development and $16,000 to Kwe Kwe for construction of a self-contained housing unit: a home and school for children orphaned by AIDS. The club's contribution to the Himalayan project garnered a matching amount from RI. That larger amount was then matched by the Canadian International Development Association (CIDA) for a total of $80,000.

Meanwhile, Alf Savage had established The Rotary Club of Calgary as a recognized applicant for Alberta's Wild Rose Foundation grants. The club's Kwe Kwe contribution was matched by Wild Rose and matched again by CIDA to produce $72,000 for the orphan home.

In 1995–96, Garth Toombs's year as president, Roger Brett travelled to Kwe Kwe and came back with another Zimbabwean project: a hospital trauma unit in Kadoma. In 1996, the club invested $15,000 there.

The club became increasingly resourceful. When it discovered that used medical equipment could be purchased in Canada, it bought enough for a 1998 shipment to Sierra Leone. The equipment was distributed to two government hospitals and a medical training centre. Wheelchairs and walkers were presented to homes for senior citizens.

As the century and millennium closed, the club was contributing to projects in Guatemala (home for girls), southern India (comfort stations), Uganda (water), Zimbabwe (wheelchairs), and Peru (training of the handicapped). In 2000–01, it added a maternity hospital in Russia, earthquake relief for Turkey, an Operation Eyesight Universal clinic in Peru, and a project to buy bicycles for Thai children so they could get to school.

The international work done by clubs like The Rotary Club of Calgary was having powerful effects in the developing nations. Within Rotary itself, an interesting side effect was the amount of club-to-club and multi-club partnering that was going on. In 2001–02, The Rotary Club of Calgary contributed to a South American micro-credit project led by the Calgary West Club; also a school latrines project in the Dominican Republic led by Calgary Chinook. Partnering also occurred city to city. For example, in 2003, a team of Calgary pediatricians led by Dr. Jim Harder went to Ecuador to perform surgeries. The Riverview Rotary Club of Edmonton sponsored the trip, and The Rotary Club of Calgary contributed to project expenses.

The club's international budget continued to increase. Between 1991 and 2004, it rose from $5,000 to $45,000.

THE YEAR 2005 MARKED the one-hundredth anniversary of Rotary. As it approached, clubs were looking for legacy projects worthy of the occasion. But tragic events around the world at that time meant there were more immediate needs for Rotary funds.

On December 26, 2004, an undersea earthquake in the Indian Ocean created enormous tsunamis that swamped seaside and island communities. Over 230,000 people were killed and millions more were left homeless. The Rotary Club of Calgary put Jack Lamarsh in charge of its relief fund. His committee set a goal of $50,000 and named the fund after James Wheeler Davidson, recognizing that many tsunami-stricken communities were ones he had visited on behalf of Rotary.

RI was well placed to help with the relief of Thailand: Rotary had four Districts in that country — and a former RI President, Mr. Bichai Ratikul. Mr. Ratikul led a Rotary initiative to rebuild homes and infrastructure. The Rotary Club of Calgary partnered with the Rotary Club of Bangkok to rebuild two villages in Krabi province. The mix of donors included clubs from Thailand, the U.S., and Canada, and a memorial was erected in Thailand to recognize the successful partnership.

Rotary mounted a second relief drive in September of its centennial year for the U.S. Gulf Coast and New Orleans, ravished by Hurricane Katrina. The club cooperated with World Community Service and District 6200 in Louisiana. Guatemalan victims of Hurricane Stan were almost forgotten in the shadow of the massive Louisiana and Southeast Asian catastrophes, but the club sent $5,000 to help the people of Guatemala rebuild.

THE ROTARY CLUB OF CALGARY'S RELIEF WORK in Asia, the southern U.S., and Guatemala would have been sufficient to honour the club's centennial, but the club still wanted a legacy project. When Walter Haessel was chosen to chair the club's World Community Service Committee in 2005, Bill Redmond, club president, came to Walter with a problem, or an opportunity, depending how you looked at it. The club's major donation for the year was to be Rotary Challenger Park, but fundraising had gone so well that the two-year commitment had been met in the first year. Now the club wanted a new project, a signature *international* legacy project, for which it could fundraise. Hence, the board had agreed to add to the World Community Service budget, bringing it abruptly to $195,000. It had been $45,000 the year before.

Walter's jaw fell. An increase in budget that massive should be studied by a new committee. Time was needed. Bill Redmond said there was no time.

Club member Bruce Fenwick recommended that Walter look into CAWST, an inventive clean-water initiative pioneered at the University of Calgary. Bruce was a CAWST board member. CAWST, the Centre for Affordable Water and Sanitation Technology, traced back to 1998, when Camille Dow Baker left a career in oil and gas to study environmental design at the University of Calgary. There she met Dr. David Manz, the inventor of a household water treatment device called the Biosand filter. Together they founded CAWST. Although the Biosand filter was excellent technology, CAWST's emphasis was on training people in developing countries to implement water quality and sanitation programs. The Biosand filter was one means to that end.

At the time that Walter Haessel approached CAWST, the centre had a long list of organizations throughout the developing world trained to build the Biosand filter and improve local sanitation. The problem was that all these organizations needed money to implement the program. CAWST's suggestion was that Rotary provide $5,000 to a number of these groups. "We're not a cheque-writing club," Walter remembers telling CAWST. The club wanted bigger projects in which its members could get involved. "We wanted to get our hands dirty."

In the end, three international CAWST projects became the club's centennial legacy. The club provided seed money for the building of Biosand filters and the implementation of well and latrine projects in Cambodia and Indonesia. The Indonesian project was led by club member Lloyd Flood who had lengthy experience working in Indonesia

and spoke the Bahassa language. The third project, again focused on Biosand filters, was in Uganda. Tex Tychon, a former Canadian who lived there, led this one.

All three projects were so successful that The Rotary Club of Calgary decided to continue supporting CAWST. The club's 2006 New Year's Eve Gala was a fundraiser for CAWST. The club changed the guest speaker's gift at luncheons. From now on, the gift would be a Biosand filter bought in the speaker's name.

When asked what the biggest transition has been in The Rotary Club of Calgary's international work, Walter Haessel points to Bill Redmond's decision to lever up the international budget in 2005 — and find projects to match it. Instead of being a one-shot deal, the move raised the club's international spending to a higher threshold, and kept it there.

Meanwhile, at CAWST, those in charge of the centre were not satisfied with its progress. They felt they were not gaining on the world's water and sanitation problems. Rather than work from Calgary, they wanted to develop Water Expertise Training Centres (WET Centres) in the countries where the problems existed. CAWST had CIDA funding but needed more. The Rotary Club of Calgary committed seed money to help leverage funds for WET Centres in Haiti, Nepal, and Zambia. In just two years, the program trained 645 organizations and improved water and sanitation for 88,000 households (529,000 people). For the Africa Manzi WET Centre project in Zambia, both the WET Centre's organizers and CAWST received a National Energy Globe Award.

CAWST's next approach to The Rotary Club of Calgary was to ask for seed money for an $8 million follow-up project: the development of WET Centres in eight more countries. That project is proceeding.

• • •

IN ITS INTERNATIONAL WORK, The Rotary Club of Calgary has brought in a system of "champions," whereby individuals in the club take responsibility for a project or group of projects and focus their energies there.

Tom Loucks and Walter Haessel have become the club champions for the Cambodia CAWST project. Walter took the CAWST training course and has visited Pursat, Cambodia, nine times. He and Tom Loucks have seen the involvement of The Rotary Club of Calgary expand beyond water and sanitation to include agricultural development, health care, and micro-finance for education. In the second half of the 1970s, the Khmer Rouge left Pursat devastated. Villages were depopulated and starving, and The Rotary Club of Calgary's projects are part of rebuilding the community.

Walter Haessel has led many Rotary groups on tours of Pursat, which has drawn other clubs into supporting Rotary work at Pursat or leading projects of their own. After the RI Conference in Bangkok in 2012, forty-eight Rotarians from around the world travelled to Pursat, twenty-three of them Albertans.

THE CURLY GALBRAITH GLOBAL MEMORIAL

Many in The Rotary Club of Calgary wanted to set up a memorial project in the name of past RI Director Curly Galbraith. The project, called the Curly Galbraith Global Memorial, provides scholarships to help AIDS orphans attend university. The club approved its charter in April 2011. Garth and Ann Toombs co-chaired the project. Doris Galbraith and her family made major initial donations. Thanks to this program, in 2013, twenty-five AIDS orphans attended university in Uganda.

Another of the club's international champions is Garth Toombs. In 2001, following a visit to India, Toombs sponsored a rain-harvesting project in Southern India, to which Calgary Rotary donated $20,000 (matched by the Wild Rose Foundation and The Rotary Foundation). The project provided 268 water-harvesting units for homes. Besides proving the effectiveness of this technology, the work also created a new industry: local people in Southern India were skilled enough in building concrete rooftop water-harvesting units to do this for their living.

In 2004, at the urging of Charles Pratt, Garth visited Uganda and returned with thirty-eight Rotary project proposals, many of which were picked up by District Rotary Clubs. While in Uganda, Garth met a Ugandan Rotarian who presented a project to assist orphans living in child-headed homes. In 2006, Garth and his wife Ann visited Uganda to assess the needs of clubs in Masaka, Kalisizo, and Kyotera. The project chosen helped child heads of families. Garth and Ann also suggested providing micro-credit to people affected by AIDS.

THE ROTARY CLUB OF CALGARY prefers direct action to cheque-writing in its international service projects. In Pursat, Cambodia, club members have been improving water and sanitation through Biosand filters and rain harvest since 2005.

The project, now known as TRACC (Taking Rotary Assistance to Communities and Children), assists approximately five hundred orphans and five hundred micro-credit recipients. The Rotary Club of Calgary's contribution to TRACC is $55,000, to date. The Rotary Foundation, The Canadian Rotary Collaboration for International Development, other Rotary Clubs, and personal donations have contributed well over $1.5 million.

Many projects grew out of TRACC, including sending four shipping containers of used medical equipment to hospitals in the area. Seventy-five thousand books were sent via the Africa Book Project. There were also special needs projects: rebuilding homes, building latrines, and providing orphans with bicycles.

• • •

THE ROTARY CLUB OF CALGARY'S RECORD of international accomplishment was threatened by the banking

crisis and financial collapse of 2008. The aftermath of this disaster reduced revenues at a time when the club had many commitments. These were challenging times, but the club discovered it had a depth of talent, resources, and strategies to deal with them. It did not default on any of its commitments.

Though the club's expenditure on international service projects was drastically reduced between 2008 and 2011, veteran international schemers like Charles Pratt, Garth Toombs, and Walter Haessel managed to shore up the club's projects with individual member donations and matching grants.

As The Rotary Club of Calgary's centennial year approached, the club remained a strong player in international service. Garth Toombs and Walter Haessel were awarded RI's Service Above Self Award, an honour bestowed on no more than 150 Rotarians per year in the entire Rotary world.*

• • •

* Carl Smith and Phil Libin have also received the Service Above Self Award.

ROTARY INTERNATIONAL MALARIA PROJECT

In 2007, Charles Pratt championed a major multi-year project to provide treated bed nets to children in fourteen countries in East Africa where malaria is epidemic. More African children die from malaria than any other cause. Charles has convinced many clubs beyond The Rotary Club of Calgary to help fund the project, which has benefitted also from the support of the Rotary Foundation through matching and global grants. He has received many accolades for this work.

IF A PERSON WITH NO KNOWLEDGE of The Rotary Club of Calgary were to read about its first fifty years and then be asked to guess what the club went on to do in its next fifty years, that person might correctly predict that the club went on to bigger and bigger contributions to its city. It is much less likely that the person would correctly predict the huge amount of international work the club has undertaken.

The international work required a change of thinking about what a Rotary Club in a western Canadian city should be trying to do with its growing financial power, and that change of thinking is the final story in this book because it is the newest powerful development in the maturation of this one-hundred-year-old club. The change is very much rooted in one's own emotional feeling about the word "community." Is your community the four-block radius around your house? Is it your side of the river? Is it Calgary as a whole, Alberta as a whole, Canada as a whole? Or is it the entire world?

This sense that the whole world is one's community is where Rotary has been pointing ever since World War II. But the response from The Rotary Club of Calgary was nonetheless an exercise of the club's free will. The degree that the club has added the international sphere to its service commitment has been determined by the membership. When it comes to the international work of the club, the membership is excited, committed, and ready for more.

It is The Rotary Club of Calgary itself that wants to improve water and sanitation in the developing world. Toward those ends, the club has participated singly and in partnership in all of the following countries: Guatemala, Cambodia, Uganda, Thailand, Malawi, Tanzania, Haiti, Nepal, Afghanistan, Indonesia, and Ecuador — and not even that long list is complete.

CONCLUSION

ONE HUNDRED YEARS OF COMMUNITY SERVICE: 1914 to 2014! Hundreds of Rotary Club of Calgary members working around the calendar in the service of others — this is The Rotary Club of Calgary's accomplishment. It is the spirit celebrated by this book.

The motto "Service Above Self" is a mystery, something each member must solve for his or her own self. Hundreds of members engaged with one another, engaged with Rotarian families around the world, seeking to live up to that motto is a force that can accomplish almost anything. Rotary's PolioPlus campaign is a fine example. Rotarians set what many considered an impossible goal: the eradication of a terrible disease. While polio resisted total eradication, the campaign made enormous strides, a 99 percent reduction in new cases. Rotary Club of Calgary members put their all into that campaign, and

Rotary wife Verneil Martin added over $1 million to the drive with her cookbook *Among Friends*. That is the power of Rotary.

The club's financial strength has grown over time. Donations and bequests from club members increased the club's endowment, extending its potential while buffering against economic cycles. This has allowed the club to greatly expand its international programs and to employ the savvy and experience of Calgary members. Improvements in sanitation, clean water, malaria reduction, and support for HIV orphans are the results.

While performing service for their own and other communities, club members and their families have had a lot of fun. They have made friends in ways that do not tarnish or tire, or harm anyone. They have made friends around the world.

SERVICE IN ROTARY INTERNATIONAL

A number of members of The Rotary Club of Calgary have gone on to serve Rotary International: as District governors, RI Board members, and RI vice-presidents. A member does not have to work for RI to make a mark for Rotary, but still there is a pride among club members when one of their number moves on to help lead the parent club.

The Rotary Club of Calgary has yet to provide a president for RI, but it has come close. Curly Galbraith was the nearest, when he was RI vice-president in 1989–90. James Wheeler Davidson was third vice-president in the 1920s as was Glen Peacock in the 1950s. Others members of The Rotary Club of Calgary, besides Curly Galbraith, Glen Peacock, and James Wheeler Davidson, have served as RI directors: Jeff Lydiatt in 1922–23 and Bill Gant in 1993–94. Members who have served as District governor include Jim Ryan, James Wheeler Davidson, Frank Freeze, Fred Osborne, Glen Peacock, Harry Hays, Bill Gillott, Curly Galbraith, Vinny Jacques, Doug Martin, Steve Allan, Bill Gant, and Garth Toombs (2014–15).

The Rotary Club of Calgary was the first Rotary Club in Calgary. Now, there are thirteen. The original club has helped spark and sponsor many of those clubs — as well as ones elsewhere in its District and the world. The club represents a great history and a powerful will. Wherever it focuses its vision, improvements blossom. This is the tradition members of The Rotary Club of Calgary carry into the future.

● ● ●

ONE HUNDRED YEARS — ONE HUNDRED PRESIDENTS

1914: James Ryan
(became District governor)
1915: Wilkie. G. Fowler
1916: Dr. George W. Kerby
1917: Jeff Lydiatt
(became RI director)
1918: Lon Cavanaugh
1919: James W. Davidson
(became RI director and third vice-president of RI)
1920: Bill Marshall
1921: Fred Osborne
(became District governor)
1922: Pete Naismith
1923: Fred Shouldice
1924: Rueban Ward
1925: Charles Smith
1926: George Hutton
1927: Fred Spooner
1928: Frank Freeze
(became District governor)
1929: Arthur McGuire
1930: David Black
1931: T. Alex Hornibrook
1932: Ernie. L. Richardson
1933: George Hughes
1934: Bill MacArthur
1935: Walter Davidson
1936: Jack McMurchy
1937: Alex Ross

1938: Doug Howland
1939: Maurice Brown
1940: Dr. W. Lincoln
1941: Fred Stapells
1942: Matt Brownlee
1943: Russell Allen
1944: Sam Coultis
1945: Frank Mirtle
1946: Bill Knights
1947: James Fowler
1948: Ernest Peterson
1949: Bill Snaddon
1950: Glen Peacock
(became RI director and third vice-president of RI)
1951: Harold Morkill
1952: Charlie Kennedy
1953: Ron Jenkins
1954: Leishman McNeill
1955: Glen Elder
1956: Bert Dyson
1957: John Stevenson
1958: Harry Hays
(became District governor)
1959: James Mahaffy
1960: Merv Cozart
1961: Charles Pinnell
1962: Fred McKinnon
1963: Holland Cameron
1964: Myrl Courtwright

1965: Fane Polley
1966: George Bateman
1967: Owen Funnell
1968: Bill Tait
1969: Kelly Gibson
1970: Curly Galbraith
(became RI director and vice-president of RI)
1971: Jim Fowler
1972: George Morrison
1973: Howard Paillefer
1974: George Robbins
1975: Jack Illsey
1976: Vinny Jacques
(became District governor)
1977: Don Telfer
1978: Jim McKibben
1979: Joe Brager
1980: Don Campbell
1981: Tom Walsh
1982: Doug Martin
(became District governor)
1983: Gordon Anderson
1984: Dawn Fairbairn
1985: Stan Sailer
1986: Bill Gant
(became District governor and RI director)
1987: Bill Kaufmann
1988: Chuck Simpson

1989: Richard Copithorne
1990: Gordon Walker
1991: Terry McMahon
1992: Bill Gillott
(became District governor)
1993: Bob Junker
1994: Steve Allan
(became District governor)
1995: Garth Toombs
(became District governor)
1996: George Brookman
1997: Hank Popoff
1998: John Hogan
1999: John Bertagnolli
2000: Jim Denis
2001: John Boyd
2002: Jack Lamarsh
2003: Tony Howard
2004: Jim Shaner
2005: Bill Redmond
2006: Bill Walsh
2007: Michael Broadhurst
2008: Roy Boettger
2009: Larry Shelley
2010: Bill Keech
2011: Bruce Fenwick
2012: Doug MacDonald
2013: Eva Friesen

SELECTED SOURCES

Paul P. Harris, *Honoring Our Past: The Words and Wisdom of Paul Harris*, Rotary International, 1986.

Dr. Robert J. Lampard, *The Life and Times of James and Lillian Davidson in Rotary International*, Rotary Club of Red Deer, 2006.

Verneil Martin, *Among Friends*, Among Friends Publishing, Limited, 1989.

Peter Penner, *Manchester to Calgary South, 1955–2005: Rotary Fellowship in Action*, Rotary Club of Calgary South, 2004.

Donald B. Smith, *Calgary's Grand Story: The Making of a Prairie Metropolis from the Viewpoint of Two Heritage Buildings*, University of Calgary Press, 2005.

Cecil "Swanny" Swanson, *The Days of My Sojourning*, Calgary-Alberta Institute, 1977.

Jefferey Williams, *Far From Home*, University of Calgary Press, 2003.

IMAGE CREDITS

vi: Michel Berdnikoff

viii: Heather Simonds

x: The Rotary Club of Calgary

xii: Michel Berdnikoff

xvi: Doris Galbraith

2: Nan Walker Jensen

3: Heather Simonds

4: Glenbow Archives NA-2345-1

5. The Rotary Club of Calgary, photo by Heather Simonds

6: John Reed – Rotary Club of Jersey, Channel Islands

8: (L) Glenbow Archives NA-254-23, (R) Glenbow Archives NA-967-12

8: (Top) Glenbow Archives NA-2059-34; (Bottom) Heather Simonds

10: Heather Simonds

11: Glenbow Archives NA-2562-2

12: Glenbow Archives NA-2768-4

15: Glenbow Archives ND-3-5812i

17: (Top left) Glenbow Archives NA-1494-30, (Right) Glenbow Archives NA-1494-34, (Bottom left), Edworthy Family

20: Glenbow Archives A-2019-3

23: (Top) Glenbow Archives NA-5600-7772a, (Bottom) Glenbow Archives M-1700-108-1

24: The Rotary Club of Calgary

26: Glenbow Archives PB-355-3

27: The Rotary Club of Calgary

28: Heather Simonds

29: The Rotary Club of Calgary

32: Glenbow Archives NA-3766-1

33: Glenbow Archives NA-2345-4

34: The Rotary Club of Calgary

37: University of Calgary Archives 2012.004_15.03

38: (Top) University of Calgary Archives 2012.004_15.06, (Bottom) University of Calgary Archives 2012.004_15.04

39: University of Calgary Archives, 2012.004_15.07

41: Photo of painting taken by Heather Simonds

42: Glenbow Archives NA-2345-25

44: Glenbow Archives NA-2345-56

46: (Left) Glenbow Archives M-9553-87-2, (Right) Glenbow Archives M-9553-86-1

47: (Top) Michel Berdnikoff, (Bottom) Heather Simonds

48: Heather Simonds

50: Glenbow Archives M-7841-305-2

51: Glenbow Archives M-9553-95-1

52: (Top) The Rotary Club of Calgary; (Bottom) Glenbow Archives PA-2079-30

54: Glenbow Archives PA-2079-38

56: The Rotary Club of Calgary

60: Heather Simonds

62: Heather Simonds

64: Glenbow Archives M-9553-78

65: Glenbow Archives NA-2377-1

72: Glenbow Archives M-1700-101-1

74: Glenbow Archives M-9553-2-1a

76: Glenbow Archives M-9553-58-1

77: (Top) Glenbow Archives M-9553-59-1, (Bottom) Glenbow Archives M-9553-59-2

78: (Top left) Glenbow Archives M-9553-54-4, (Top Right) Glenbow Archives M-955358-3, (Bottom) Glenbow Archives M-9553-54-1

79: Glenbow Archives M-9553-58-2

80: Glenbow Archives PA-2079-28

81 to 91: Heather Simonds

92: Glenbow Archives M-9553-90-4

93: Glenbow Archives M-9553-81-2

94: Heather Simonds

95: Mayhood Estate

99: Glenbow Archives NA-2768-2

100: Glenbow Archives M-9553-110-1

101: Glenbow Archives M-7841-29-8

102: Glenbow Archives M-7841-300-1

103: The Rotary Club of Calgary

104: The Rotary Club of Calgary, photo by Heather Simonds

105: The Rotary Club of Calgary

108: Dr. Marmie Hess

109: Jo-Ann Clarke

111: (Left) Glenbow Archives M-7841-300-2, (Right) Glenbow Archives M-9553-54-2

112: (Top) Glenbow Archives M-9553-54-3, (Bottom) The Rotary Club of Calgary, photo taken by Heather Simonds

113: Nan Walker Jensen

114: The Rotary Club of Calgary

119: (Left) Glenbow Archives PA-2453-228, (Right) Glenbow Archives PA-2079-x

120: (Left: Top and Bottom) Heather Simonds, (Right) Glenbow Archives M-1700-110-1

121: Ann Toombs

122: The Rotary Club of Calgary

124: The Rotary Club of Calgary

126: The Rotary Club of Calgary

127: (Left) The Rotary Club of Calgary, (Right) Garth Toombs

128: The Rotary Club of Calgary

INDEX